Meyer Kayserling, Charles M. Parr, Ruth Parr

Christopher Columbus and the participation of the Jews in the Spanish and Portuguese discoveries

Meyer Kayserling, Charles M. Parr, Ruth Parr

Christopher Columbus and the participation of the Jews in the Spanish and Portuguese discoveries

ISBN/EAN: 9783337147808

Printed in Europe, USA, Canada, Australia, Japan

Cover: Foto ©ninafisch / pixelio.de

More available books at **www.hansebooks.com**

CHRISTOPHER COLUMBUS

CHRISTOPHER COLUMBUS

AND

THE PARTICIPATION OF THE JEWS IN THE
SPANISH AND PORTUGUESE DISCOVERIES

BY

Dr. M. KAYSERLING

TRANSLATED FROM THE AUTHOR'S MANUSCRIPT WITH HIS SANCTION
AND REVISION

By CHARLES GROSS, Ph.D.
ASST. PROFESSOR OF HISTORY, HARVARD COLLEGE

NEW YORK
LONGMANS, GREEN, AND CO.
1894

COPYRIGHT, 1894, BY
LONGMANS, GREEN, AND CO.

Press of J. J. Little & Co.
Astor Place, New York

DEDICATED

TO

MR. LAZARUS STRAUS,

OF NEW YORK,

AS A TOKEN OF ESTEEM, AND IN RECOGNITION OF HIS
ENCOURAGING INTEREST IN THE RESEARCHES
CONTAINED IN THIS BOOK.

PREFACE.

FEW mortals have been honored by posterity as much as Christopher Columbus, though during his life-time the discoverer of a New World received little credit for his achievements. Monuments of Columbus have been erected in Genoa, proud to call him her son; in Barcelona, where after his first voyage to America the Spanish sovereigns received him with great rejoicing and with princely honors; in Valladolid, where he died; in Seville, Madrid, Huelva, New York, San Domingo, and in many other cities of Italy, Spain, and America. His praises have been sung in odes and ballads, and his name has been glorified by dramatist and novelist.

And in our day, four hundred years after the discovery of America, his achievements have been most worthily commemorated by the academies and learned societies of all nations. To honor his name Spain has just held the great *Exposición Historico-Europea* in Madrid; and America has just closed the Chicago Exhibition, which attracted millions of visitors. The Church has canonized him. In synagogues and temples his services in promoting the social and commercial intercourse of nations, and especially in advancing nautical and geographical science, have been recognized and lauded. In the just appreciation of his great services to mankind, all political, religious, and social differences have vanished.

The commemoration of his achievements has also materially enriched historical literature. His descent, his education, his voyages and discoveries, all the events of his life, have recently been investigated and described. In doing this, writers have regarded his life from different points of view. Some of his biographers have even seen in his career not the triumph of science but that of religion; and a learned Spaniard has in all seriousness asserted that without his strong religious faith Columbus would never have discovered America.* For a long time Isabella, the pious Queen of Castile, received credit for being the chief or sole promoter of his expeditions and discoveries. In recent times Aragonese writers have, however, disputed the justice of this claim, and, to maintain their national honor, have ascribed to their king, Ferdinand the Catholic, an equal share in the promotion of Columbus's plans. More or less justice has also been done to the other per-

---

* S. de la Rósa y López, *El Libros y Autografos de D. Chr. Colón* [Seville, 1891].

sons who helped him and who directly or indirectly participated in his discoveries.

The question whether the Jews assisted in these discoveries has already heretofore been propounded,* but it has never before been carefully investigated. The credit of having given the first impulse to the present work belongs to one of the most public-spirited citizens of America, the venerable Mr. Lazarus Straus, and to his son, Hon. Oscar S. Straus of New York, formerly minister of the United States in Turkey and since 1892 president of the American Jewish Historical Society. Entrusted with this honorable but difficult mission, I determined to visit Spain in order to complete my collection of material by exploring the Spanish archives and libraries. Such documents as I found there, I transcribed. They have been used with care in the text, and are printed *in extenso* in the Appendix.

My investigations in Spain were greatly facili-

---

* This was done thirty-six years ago by the writer of the present work in an article entitled *Die portugiesischen Entdeckungen und Eroberungen in Beziehung zu den Juden*, in *Monatsschrift für Geschichte und Wissenschaft des Judenthums* [Edited by Z. Frankel], vii. 433-446; *Jahrbuch für die Geschichte der Juden und des Judenthums*, vol. iii. According to C. P. Daly's *Settlement of the Jews in North America* [2d edition by M. J. Kohler, New York, 1893], Rev. Dr. K. Kohler delivered an address on this subject before the German Historical Society of New York; it was printed in the *Belletristisches Journal*, May, 1891.

tated by the kindness of Spanish officials and *savants*, and by the praiseworthy liberality with which the authorities of the archives at Alcalá de Henares, Barcelona, Madrid, Seville, and other places allowed me to use their manuscript treasures. My warm thanks are due particularly to certain Spanish investigators, who are well known far beyond the boundaries of Spain—to the learned and ever-obliging R. P. Fidel Fita (who has made many valuable contributions to the history of Spain), the excellent historian D. Victor Balaguer, the distinguished student of Columbus literature D. Cesáreo Fernández Duro, the amiable D. Jerónimo López de Ayala, Vizconde de Palazuelos, D. Ramón Santa María, and to several other gentlemen in Barcelona, Madrid, Seville, and Saragossa.

It only remains for me to add a few words of explanation regarding the Marranos, or secret Jews, and their status. The terrible massacres of 1391 and later persecutions had compelled or induced vast numbers of Jews to submit to baptism. The great majority of these converts adhered to Judaism more firmly than is commonly supposed. Though they had succumbed to force (*anussim*) and had become Christians in appearance or outwardly, they lived according to the precepts and laws of their ancestral faith. In the city of

Seville, a Jewish chronicle * informs us, an inquisitor thus addressed the king: "Sire, if you wish to ascertain how the *anussim*, or secret Jews, observe the Sabbath, let us ascend this tower. Behold there the house of a pseudo-Christian, yonder is another, and here are several more. However cold the weather may be, you would not see smoke rising from any of these dwellings, for it is the Sabbath, and on that day the secret Jews allow no fire to be kindled. They also have a man who slaughters animals for them according to Jewish rites and brings the meat to their houses, and another who performs circumcision."

That Jewish writers have not exaggerated the loyalty of the Marranos to their ancestral religion is proven by the countless victims of the Inquisition in Spain and Portugal and in the Spanish and Portuguese colonies who during the three centuries of its existence died in dungeons or on the funeral pile. Their religious loyalty will not be fully recognized and appreciated before the enormous mass of documentary evidence in the state archives of Alcalá de Henares and Simancas and in several archives of Portugal has been sifted and utilized. Until quite recent times this material was wholly or in great part neglected.

I trust that I have succeeded in making a

---

* Shevet Jehuda [ed. Wiener], number 64, p. 96.

contribution to the history of the discovery of America and to the history of the Jews, to whom America has been a land of refuge, a land of freedom and of equality.*

M. KAYSERLING.

BUDAPEST, *October*, 1893.

---

* [The translator is greatly obliged to Mr. and Mrs. Emanuel Cohen of Minneapolis, Minn., for assistance in reading the proof-sheets of this volume.]

CONTENTS.

CHAPTER I.

	PAGES
THE JEWS AND THE SPANISH NAVY	1–3
THE JEWS AND THE PORTUGUESE NAVY	4–5
JEHUDA CRESQUES, OR JAIME RIBES	5–8
JOÃO II. AND HIS ASTRONOMICAL JUNTA	9–10

CHAPTER II.

COLUMBUS IN LISBON	11–13
HIS SCIENTIFIC EQUIPMENT	13–15
HIS NEGOTIATIONS WITH JOÃO II.	15–17
JOSEPH VECINHO	17–18
PORTUGUESE EXPEDITION TO INDIA	18
ABRAHAM OF BEJA AND JOSEPH ZAPATEIRO	18–20
COLUMBUS IN SPAIN	20–21

CHAPTER III.

POLITICAL CONDITION OF ARAGON AND CASTILE	22–24
FERDINAND AND ISABELLA	24–25
ABRAHAM SENIOR	25–27
STATUS OF JEWS AND MARRANOS	27–31
THE INQUISITION	31–40

CHAPTER IV.

	PAGES
Columbus at the Spanish Court	41–43
The Junta of Cordova	43–45
The Conference at Salamanca	45–46
Abraham Zacuto	46–51
Isaac Abravanel	52–54

CHAPTER V.

Columbus in Santa Fé	55–57
The Fall of Granada	57–58
The Santangels	59–66
The Santangels and the Inquisition	66–69
Luis de Santangel	69–72
His Plea in behalf of Columbus	72–74
The Queen's Jewels	74–76
Santangel's Loan	77–79

CHAPTER VI.

Expulsion of the Jews from Spain	80–85
Agreement of Santa Fé	85–86
Exodus of the Jews	87–88
Jews in Columbus's Fleet	89–90
Guanahani	91–93
Luis de Torres	93–95
Indians and Israelites	95–99

CHAPTER VII.

Columbus's Return	100
His Letters to Santangel and Sanchez	100–103

CONTENTS.

	PAGES
THE JEWS AND COLUMBUS'S SECOND VOYAGE	103–111
VASCO DA GAMA AND ABRAHAM ZACUTO	111–113
GASPAR DA GAMA	113–119
ALBUQUERQUE AND HUCEFE	119–121

CHAPTER VIII.

COLUMBUS'S DOWNFALL	122–123
ROYAL FAVORS GRANTED TO SANTANGEL	123–125
DEATH OF SANTANGEL AND SANCHEZ	125
THEIR DESCENDANTS	125–126
MARRANOS IN ESPAÑOLA AND IN OTHER COLONIES	126–129
THE INQUISITION IN THE COLONIES	129–134

APPENDIX.

THE SANTANGELS	135–152
INDIANS AND ISRAELITES	153–156
THE JEWS AND COLUMBUS'S SECOND VOYAGE	157–169
QUEEN JUANA AND THE MARRANOS OF ESPAÑOLA	169–171

CHRISTOPHER COLUMBUS.

CHAPTER I.

The Earliest Participation of the Jews in the Naval Affairs of Spain and Portugal—Jehuda Cresques, or Jaime Ribes—João II. and his Astronomical Junta.

Owing to their favorable geographical situation, Spain and Portugal early became prominent maritime powers. Their discoveries and conquests in the fifteenth and sixteenth centuries astonished the world, and turned its history into new channels. The Spaniards, particularly the people of Catalonia and Aragon, were especially active in maritime affairs. Their shipping and foreign trade developed so rapidly that they rivalled, and, in fact, soon surpassed, the mercantile marine of Venice, Pisa, and Genoa, the older commercial cities of Italy.

As early as the beginning of the thirteenth century, Barcelona's commerce with Alexandria, the capital and chief seaport of Egypt, and with the north coast of Africa, was of great importance, in spite of papal prohibitions. Even in the middle of the twelfth century the Jewish traveller Benjamin of Tudela, the predecessor of Marco Polo, mentions the prosperity of Barcelona. To inform himself concerning his co-religionists he had visited the greater part of Southern Europe, of Africa, and of Asia, and his well-known book of travels was translated into many languages. He describes Barcelona as a beautiful city, frequented by merchants from all lands—from Greece and Italy, from Egypt and Palestine, and from other neighboring parts of Asia. Ships bearing the Aragonian and Catalonian flag soon traversed the African seas, and reached Egypt and Syria. During several centuries the maritime enterprises and conquests of Aragon gave her a prominent place among the European powers.

The Jews rendered noteworthy services in connection with the marine development of Spain. R. Jehuda of Valencia, or, as he was called by contemporary historians, Don Jehudano, the richest Jew of Aragon, was the confidential friend and the treasurer of King Jaime I., who asked his advice in the most important affairs of state. In 1263, at the request of the king, he fitted out a fleet which was placed in command of the Infante Don Fernando Sanchez, and three years later Jehuda was intrusted with the preparations for the conquest of Murcia.* In 1323, when Don Alfonso, the heir-apparent of the crown of Aragon, fitted out a great fleet for the conquest of Cerdeña, Tortosa showed more patriotic zeal than any other city in the kingdom. The rich Jewish community of that town, at its own expense, equipped and manned two galleys. Before the fleet sailed, King Jaime II. assured the Jews of Tortosa of his gratitude and good-will.† Moreover, the Jews of Aragon soon participated in maritime affairs personally, as well as financially. To mention only one example, Juceff Faquin, a Jew of Barcelona, "had navigated the whole then known world," as King Jaime III., the last king of Mallorca, himself testifies in 1334.‡

As in Aragon, so also in Castile the Jews contributed to the development of the navy. When King Sancho IV. formed a plan to wrest Tarifa from the Moors, he found that he had not money enough to equip his fleet. In this emergency Don Juda, treasurer of the queen Maria de Molina, lent him twenty thousand maravedis in gold. Without this assistance the king could not have

---

* Tourtoulon, *Jacme I. le Conquérant*, liv. 4, cap. 3 ; Balaguer, *Historia de Cataluña*, liv. 6, cap. 12 ; *Archivo de la Corona de Aragon*, Reg. 12, fol. 17.

† Balaguer, liv. 7, cap. 11 ; *Archivo de la Corona de Aragon*, Reg. 224, fol. 119.

‡ *Revue des Études Juives*, iv. 53 sq.

undertaken the expedition, and it would have been necessary to postpone the conquest of Tarifa.*

The first ruler of Portugal who promoted the development of a navy was Sancho II., whose reign marks the beginning of that country's maritime activity. The Jews of the kingdom were soon required to furnish an anchor, and a new cable sixty ells long, for every new ship fitted out by the crown (the so-called " fleet-tax "); and, already in early times, they were employed in the naval service.† Under King João I. discoveries and conquests began along the African coast. Ceuta, the seven-hilled city, the most important fortress of Mauritania, was captured in 1415, and thus the end was attained for which fame-loving princes of Portugal had long and ardently sought. On the armada which was sent to take the city, and which left Lisbon amid the plaudits of the whole population, there were also Jews, one of whom heroically died for his country in a naval engagement.‡

João I.'s third son Henry, called the Navigator,

---

* J. Amador de los Rios, *Historia de los Judíos de España y Portugal* [Madrid, 1876], ii. 61.

† Ribeiro, *Dissert.*, iii. 2, 87 sq.; Kayserling, *Gesch. der Juden in Portugal*, 55.

‡ *Chron. do Conde D. Pedro*, in *Collecção de livros ineditos da Historia Portugueza* [Lisbon, 1790], ii. 259.

had accompanied his father on the expedition against Ceuta. After the capture of the city he obtained information from Jewish travellers concerning the south coast of Guinea and the interior of Africa. This information convinced him that valuable discoveries could be made along the African coast, and that here a new route to the land of the legendary Christian king, Prester John, could be found. In his zeal to acquire new possessions for Portugal, he devoted himself wholly to navigation, and applied himself assiduously to nautical studies. He desired, above all, to provide for the thorough education of navigators, and hence he established a naval academy, or school of navigation, at the Villa do Iffante, or Sagres, a seaport town which he had caused to be built. To this school he called the most distinguished nautical scholars of his time, and appointed as its director Mestre Jaime of Mallorca.

Alexander von Humboldt in his *Cosmos* asks, Who was this Mestre Jaime? He was not Jaime Ferrer, the discoverer of Rio del Oro, as writers long supposed. Our Mestre Jaime, or James, early gained the reputation of a great mathematician, and was very skilful in the manufacture of maps and nautical instruments.* His real name was

---

* "Mestre Jacome, homem mui docto na arte de navegar, que fazia cartas e instrumentos." Barros, *Asia*, dec. 1, cap. 16.

Jafuda or Jehuda Cresques. He was the son of Abraham Cresques of Palma, the capital of Mallorca, which since the thirteenth century had been the chief seat of nautical knowledge. Here, in the home of Raymond Lull, whose *Arte de Navegar*, even in Columbus's time, was considered the best nautical treatise, cartography was a special object of study; and, as Gabriel Llabrés y Quintana, the learned vice-president of the *Luliana* in Palma, states, it was almost entirely in the hands of the Mallorcan Jews.

Jafuda Cresques was so prominent in this art, to which he had devoted himself from early youth, that the people called him *lo jueu buscoler* or *el judio de las brujelas*, " the map-Jew " or " the compass-Jew," just as his friend Moses Rimos, or Raymundo Barthomeu,* was popularly known as *el pergaminero*, " the parchment-maker." The maps of Jafuda Cresques were highly prized, not merely by navigators, but also by kings and princes. Juan I. of Aragon obtained from him a map of the world, which the king esteemed so much that he assigned a room in his palace at Barcelona for

---

* He may be identical with the Moses Rimos mentioned in Steinschneider's *Catal. MSS. Biblioth. Reg. Monachensis*, p. 36, who bought a Hebrew book in 1371. He was a kinsman of Moses Rimos, the physician and poet, who died in Sicily, at the age of twenty-four, in 1430.

its custody; and when he desired to make a present to the ruler of France, he could think of nothing more costly than this map, which is still preserved as a precious relic in the National Library in Paris. In 1387 King Juan obtained another *mapa mundi* from Jafuda at the then high price of sixty-eight pounds.*

The celebrated cosmographer, the maker of the renowned *Cataluña*, lived peacefully in his stately house in Mount Zion Street, quite near to the synagogue of Palma, until August 2, 1391, when a riot broke out which soon assumed the character of an open revolt. The furious mob attacked the Jews, who had no presentiment of impending evil, and, before the governor of the island could interfere, three hundred of them were slain. Eight hundred took refuge in the royal castle or in the university, while many others fled to the churches and were baptized. Jehuda Cresques, assuming the name of Jaime Ribes, sold his house, left the island, and by virtue of privileges granted to him by the king, with whom he stood in high favor, he settled in Barcelona, the dwelling-place of

---

* G. Llabrés y Quintana, *Boletin de la sociedad arqueológica Luliana*, 1890, p. 310 ; *Boletin de la real Academia de la Historia en Madrid*, xix. 375 sq. See also Hamy, *Cresques le Juheu, note sur un géographe juif catalan de la fin du xiv. siècle* [Paris, 1891]. Hasdai Cresques should not be confused with Jafuda Cresques.

several of his relatives—Jafuda Lobell Cresques, Solomon and Azay Cresques, and others. Here he continued to devote himself to his art, receiving employment from such persons as King Martin of Aragon, until 1438. In that year, when nearly sixty years old, he was appointed by Prince Henry director of the newly established academy at Sagres, with a large salary. This was the academy in which was laid the foundation of Columbus's projects. Mestre Jaime became the teacher of the Portuguese in the art of navigation as well as in the manufacture of nautical instruments and maps. In this work he had no superior in his day. To him we are chiefly indebted for the improvement of the compass and for the application of the astronomical astrolabe to navigation.*

From Henry the Navigator, who lived to hear of the discovery of Cape Verd and the Azores, his grand-nephew João II., who became King of Portugal in 1481, seems to have inherited a love of exploration. His attention was constantly occupied with nautical affairs; he desired, above

---

* Barros, *Asia*, dec. I, cap. 16 : " D. Henrique mandou vir Mestre Jacome, o qual lhe custou muito, pelo trazer en este Reyno pero insinar sua sciencia aos officiaes portuguezes." Candido Lusitano, *Vida do Infante D. Henrique* [Lisbon, 1758], 196 sq.; *Os Portuguezes em Africa, Asia e Oceania* [Lisbon, 1877], i. 12.

all, to provide navigators with mathematical instruments for the determination of latitude and longitude. The astrolabe, to the development of which Jewish scholars such as Abraham Ibn Esra, the physician Jacob ben Machir (also called Don Profatius), Jacob Carsoni, and others had contributed, was still imperfect; an instrument was needed by means of which the distance of a ship from the equator could be exactly computed by the varying position of the sun in the different seasons. King João requested his astronomical junta to devise some means by which navigators might, with some degree of certainty, direct their course in any part of the ocean, and thus prevent their vessels from going astray. This junta, or commission, consisted of Diogo Ortiz Castellano, Bishop of Ceuta, who acted as president, Mestre Joseph, or Joseph Vecinho,* the court physician Rodrigo, the mathematician Moses, and the Nuremberg navigator and cosmographer Martin Behaim. An epoch in the progress of nautical knowledge was made by the improvement of the astrolabe, and by the invention of a means of determining the meridian altitude of the sun—an invention by which later discoveries were facilitated and perhaps rendered possible. These

---

* Vecinho was the king's physician, an excellent mathematician and cosmographer, a pupil of Abraham Zacuto.

improvements were in great part due, as most writers admit, to Portuguese Jews.*

From the middle of the fifteenth century the Portuguese were considered the foremost navigators of the world, and their discoveries evoked general admiration. King João gladly received and patronized foreign navigators, and all who were versed in nautical affairs or in cosmography.

---

* Barros, *Asia*, dec. I, liv. 3, cap. 2 ; Telles Sylvius, *De rebus gestis Johannis* II., 90 ; Maffei, *Historia Indiarum*, 51 ; *Mem. d. Litt. Portugueza*, viii. 163.

CHAPTER II.

<small>Columbus in Lisbon, and his Relations to the Jews of that City — His Scientific Equipment — His Negotiations with King João — Joseph Vecinho — The Portuguese Expedition to India; Abraham of Beja and Joseph Zapateiro — Columbus in Spain.</small>

In 1472 a young Genoese, twenty-six years of age, proceeded to the capital of Portugal, hoping to find there the best outlet for his nautical zeal and the most rapid advancement in a maritime career. It was Cristoforo Colombo, or, to use the Latin form, Christophorus Columbus, who, after settling in Spain, called himself Colón.

Born in 1446, Columbus was the son of a poor weaver of Genoa. He spent his youth in Savona, a small maritime town, in which, as in Genoa, several Jewish families dwelt in mediæval seclusion. He and his brothers helped their father in his work, but soon Columbus followed his natural inclination, and devoted himself to navigation. Concerning his boyhood days and his education we have little authentic information; there is no historical evidence that he enjoyed the advantages of higher education, or that he attended the University of Pavia.

In 1472 we find him in Lisbon. Here, a few years later, he married Felipa Moñiz, whose grandfather was not, as some assert, of Jewish stock. Columbus was a skilful cartographer and draughtsman. He supported himself by drawing maps, in which he also dealt, just as later, in Andalusia, he traded in printed books. He was no stranger to the Jews of Lisbon. Whether he had intimate commercial relations with them, or whether in his frequent financial troubles he obtained assistance from any of them, it is difficult to determine. But we know that in his will he requested that " a half mark in silver should be paid to a Jew dwelling at the gate of the Jewry, or to him whom a priest would designate."* Long before Columbus made his will the Jews had disappeared from Lisbon.

"I have had constant relations," he himself says, "with many learned men, clergy and laymen, Jews and Moors, and many others."† He had personal intercourse with Martin Behaim, who was about the same age as Columbus, also with Joseph Vecinho (the above-mentioned mathema-

---

* " A un Judio que moraba á la puerta de la Juderia en Lisboa, ó á quien mandare un sacerdote el valor de medio marco de plata." Navarrete. *Coleccion de los Viages y Descubrimientos*, ii. 313 ; *Coleccion de Documentos inéditos de España*, xvi. 424 sq.

† *Libro de las Profecias*, fol. iv.

tician and royal physician), and with other learned Jews of Lisbon. Vecinho prepared a translation of Zacuto's astronomical tables, and gave a copy to Columbus, who, as we shall see, carried it on his travels and found it of very great service.*

During his sojourn of several years in Lisbon, which was interrupted by journeys to the coast of Guinea, Columbus worked very industriously and perseveringly to add to his meagre knowledge of mathematics and geography. In order to carry out the ambitious plans which he had formed, he devoted his attention to cosmography, philosophy, history, and similar subjects; several of his biographers say that he studied Aristotle and Duns Scotus, Pliny and Strabo, Josephus and Chronicles, the Church Fathers and the Arabian writings of the Jews. We are naturally led to inquire, What were his favorite works? What books were really in his possession?

The treatises which he studied with most zeal were Æneas Sylvius's *Historia rerum ubique gestarum* and Bishop Pierre d'Ailly's *Imago Mundi*. This latter work, it may be incidentally observed, had already in the fourteenth century been translated into Hebrew. Columbus's knowledge of

---

* It was afterwards found in his library. *Biblioteca Colombina con notas del Dr. D. Simón de la Rosa y López* [Seville, 1888], i. 3.

Aristotle, Strabo, Seneca, and other Latin and Greek classics was derived from Pierre d'Ailly's book; the *Imago Mundi* was his constant travelling companion, and his copy of it is filled with his own marginal annotations. Besides Zacuto's astronomical tables, already mentioned, he possessed some of the works written by or ascribed to Abraham Ibn Esra; for example, the little book on the "Critical Days," *Liber de luminaribus et diebus criticis*, and the *De Nativitatibus*.* Ibn Esra was an eminent man of learning; his name was honored by Christians as well as Jews. Zacuto doubtless called Columbus's attention to the *De Nativitatibus* during the latter's residence in Salamanca; he bought a copy of it in that city, according to a note in his own handwriting, for forty-one maravedis.† Later, in Spain, he read with religious zeal the tract on the Messiah, which was written by the proselyte Samuel Ibn Abbas of Morocco for the purpose of converting R. Isaac of Sujurmente; it had been translated into Spanish in 1339, and into Latin a hundred years later. This book interested Columbus so much that he excerpted

---

* It was printed in Venice in 1485 : *De Nativitatibus al reverso de la hoja primera con circulo dividido en grados y con lineas geometricas*. Venetiis, A° MCCCCLXXXV, nona Kalend. Januarii.

† These books are now in the Colombina at Seville. See *Biblioteca Colombina*, i. 3.

three whole chapters.* He was also very fond of reading the Bible and the Fourth Book of Ezra, which was probably written by a Jew who lived outside of Palestine. According to his own assertion, the incentive that impelled him to plan his discoveries was not a love of science, but his interpretation of the prophecies of Isaiah.

In Portugal Columbus earnestly conceived the idea of making maritime discoveries by way of the west. He wished to find a new ocean route to the regions of Cathay and Cipango, which were reputed to be rich in gold and spices; and also to the realm of the priest-king John, whose letter to Pope Eugene IV., or to Emperor Frederick III., a Jew is said to have first published in the middle of the fifteenth century. Henry the Navigator had already conceived a similar plan, and the Portuguese kings never lost sight of it. This bold conception took firm root in the mind of Columbus, mainly through a letter which the great Florentine physician and astrologer Toscanelli sent to King João through the monk

---

* *Libro de las Profecias*, fol. 13, in Navarrete, *Coleccion de los Viages*, ii. 260 sq.; *R. Semuel Israel [Ismael] oriundus de Civitate regis morochorum ad R. Isaac Magistrum Synagogæ quæ est in Subjulmeta, trasl. de hebreo vel de arabico in lat. p. Franc. Alfonsum Boni-Hominis, Hispanum ord. Predicatorum* [1438]. It was originally written in Arabic.

Fernando Martinez. Columbus applied to Toscanelli for a copy of this letter, and received it through Girardi, a Genoese, who was then living in Lisbon.

Columbus at length proceeded to carry out his project. He laid before King João a proposition to lead a squadron along the African coast, and thence across the ocean to the land whose wealth Marco Polo had so misleadingly described. The sullen, distrustful monarch regarded Columbus as a visionary babbler, and, especially on account of the navigator's enormous demands, saw in his scheme more pride than truth. But João laid the matter before his nautical junta, consisting of Diogo Ortiz, Bishop of Ceuta, and the court physicians Joseph and Rodrigo. They regarded the project as chimerical, and said that the whole plan rested on Columbus's visionary conception of Marco Polo's Island of Cipango.* Nevertheless the king considered the matter of such importance that he submitted it for further consideration to his council of state, in which Pedro de Menezes, Count of Villa-Real, exercised a dominant influence. Menezes thought that the exploration of the

---

* "El Rey porque via ser este Christovão Colon ... mandou que estivesse com D. Diogo Ortiz, Bispo do Ceuta, e com mestre Rodrigo e mestre Josepe, a quem elle commetia estas cousas da cosmografia." Barros, *Asia*, dec. 1, liv. 3, cap. 11.

African coast would be more conducive to the interests of Portugal, and hence he advised the king not to be misled by the visions of Columbus. In a long speech the count dwelt upon his reasons for giving this advice. His arguments were based mainly on the views of Joseph Vecinho, who was his as well as the king's physician, and whom he regarded as the highest authority in nautical matters.*

The ruler of Portugal finally refused to assist Columbus in his plans of exploration; or, as Columbus expressed it in May, 1505, in a letter to Ferdinand of Aragon, God had so stricken the king with blindness that during fourteen years he could not perceive what was desired of him.† The explorer was greatly exasperated by João's refusal, and his anger was particularly directed against "the Jew Joseph," to whom he attributed the chief blame in the miscarriage of his plans. His manuscript notes in the Colombina in Seville mention Vecinho twice. In these passages Columbus states that the King of Portugal sent his "physician and astrologer" Joseph to measure the altitude of the sun throughout Guinea, and that "the

---

* "Mestre Josepe . . . a que o Conde dava grande authoridade." Ruy de Pina, *Chron. do Conde D. Duarte*, in *Collecção de livros ineditos*, iii. 54.

† Navarrete, *Coleccion de los Viages*, iii. 528.

Jew Joseph" gave an account of this mission to the king in presence of Christopher's brother Bartholomew and many others; probably Columbus himself was also present.*

Portugal did not, however, abandon the hope of finding an ocean route to India, even without foreign aid. The wily, parsimonious king wished to turn Columbus's plans to account, without conceding any of the latter's demands. Hence, in May, 1487, he sent to the Levant two knights of his court, Affonso de Payva and Pedro de Covilhão. They departed from Lisbon with orders to seek information concerning India and the kingdom of Prester John, and they were intrusted with letters to this monarch from the Portuguese ruler. Affonso de Payva took the route to Ethiopia, and proceeded along the African coast to Sambaya, in company with a Jewish merchant whom he met on the way. The two soon be-

---

* Columbus's manuscript note in Æneas Sylvius's *Historia rerum ubique gestarum* [Venice, 1477], p. 25: "Nota quod serenissimus rex portugaliæ misit in guineam anno domini 1485 *Josephum fixicum ejus et astrologum* ad capiendum altitudinem solis in tota guinea, qui omnia adimplevit et renuntiavit dicto serenissimo regi *me presente* cum multis aliis in die xi. marcii." Manuscript note in Pierre d'Ailly's *De imagine mundi*, p. 42 : " Luego proximante a Março de 1485 cuando *el judio Josepho* hacia relacion al Rey acerca del resultado de su comision, D. Bartholomeo se hallo presente en este acto."

came intimate friends, and De Payva confided to his companion the object of his journey. Soon after their arrival in Ormuz he was stricken with a fatal illness, to the great sorrow of his Jewish friend, who solemnly promised the dying man to return to Lisbon and give the king an accurate account of all they had learned on their journey. The Jew faithfully kept his word.*

Pedro de Covilhão, for whom, at the king's command, Vecinho and Rodrigo had prepared a terrestrial globe,† visited Goa, Calicut, and Aden, and pushed onward as far as Sofala, on the east coast of South Africa. He then returned to Cairo, where he and De Payva had agreed to meet. Here he found two Jews from Portugal awaiting him, the learned Abraham of Beja and Joseph Zapateiro of Lamego. They brought the knight letters and orders from the king. Joseph had formerly visited Bagdad, and when he returned to Portugal he informed King João of what he had learned concerning Ormuz, the chief emporium for the spices of India. João requested him and the linguist Abraham to go in search of the errant Covilhão, and to direct him to send to Lisbon, through Joseph, news concerning the success of his expedition; and there-

---

* *Collecção de Documentos ineditos para a Historia das Conquistas dos Portuguezes* [Lisbon, 1858], i. 6.

† Mariz, *Dialogos*, dial. 4, cap. 10, p. 315.

after, in company with Abraham, to secure accurate information about affairs in Ormuz. Accordingly, Joseph Zapateiro joined a caravan whose goal was Aleppo, and carried back to Portugal all the information that Covilhão had gathered from Indian and Arabian mariners. The knight informed the king that, by proceeding along the west coast, the Portuguese could without difficulty reach the southern extremity of Africa. But before Joseph arrived at his destination, it was already known in Lisbon that Bartholomew Diaz had not merely discovered, but had also doubled, Cabo Tormentoso, the Cape of Good Hope.*

After his offers had been rejected by the king, Columbus resolved to leave Portugal, hoping to secure assistance elsewhere for the execution of his plans—in Genoa, in Venice, or from the King of France. His situation was indeed most wretched. He had lost his wife; he was poor, and was daily pressed by his creditors, so that he had to depart from Lisbon secretly, at night, with his little son Diego. He left Portugal in 1484, and proceeded toward Huelva, where he intended to place his child in charge of his wife's married sister. After trying in vain to induce Enrique de Guzman, the Duke of Medina-Sidonia, to cooperate with him in his projects of discovery, he

---

* Garcia de Resende, *Chron. del Rey D. João II.*, fol. 29.

applied to Luis de la Cerda, the first Duke of Medina-Celi, one of the richest princes of Andalusia. Luis, in whose veins Jewish blood flowed (his grandmother was of Jewish stock*), received him hospitably, kept him in his palace for a long time,† and seemed inclined to undertake the expedition at his own expense, especially as Columbus demanded only three or four thousand ducats in order to secure two caravels. To equip ships it was necessary, however, to obtain the assent of the crown, but permission was refused. Then the duke wrote from Rota to the queen, and on his recommendation, Columbus, after a long delay, secured access to the Spanish sovereigns, Ferdinand of Aragon and Isabella of Castile.

---

* *El Tizon de la Nobleza Española* [Barcelona, n. d.], 71.

† There is no proof that Columbus was the duke's guest for two years, as his biographers assert. In the duke's letter to the Cardinal of Spain, he says: "Yo tuve en mi casa *mucho tiempo* á C. Colón."

CHAPTER III.

Columbus in Spain—Political Condition of Aragon and Castile—Ferdinand and Isabella—Abraham Senior—Status and Political Influence of Jews and Marranos—The Inquisition and its Victims.

Columbus sought his fortune at the Spanish court during a period of violent political revolutions. It was not an opportune time for him to secure aid for his enterprise from the rulers of Spain. Discord prevailed in Castile and Aragon, in Catalonia and Navarre, and war raged along the southern frontier of the Iberian Peninsula.

Under the amiable but impotent King Henry IV., Castile had been in a condition of anarchy. On every side plots were formed by turbulent grandees, dissatisfied with the king and with his government. The crown was impoverished; even in the royal palace the most pressing wants often remained unsatisfied. The conduct of the pleasure-loving queen evoked all kinds of rumors. Beltran de la Cueva was her favorite, and the people called her daughter Beltraneja. The king, who had long been a constant object of ridicule, was at length dethroned, and his brother Alfonso was proclaimed his successor (1465).

The situation was not much better in the lands over which Juan II. of Aragon ruled. Catalonia was in arms; Aragon was threatened with the outbreak of a revolt; Navarre was the scene of bloody conflicts occasioned by the king's own son, Carlos de Viana, who claimed the right to rule on the ground that he was his mother's heir. After the death of his first wife, who was a French princess, King Juan, at the age of fifty, had married Juana Enriquez, the daughter of Fadrique Enriquez, Admiral of Castile. She was the grandchild of the beautiful Paloma, a Jewess of Toledo, and she bore the king a son, Ferdinand, whom historians call the Catholic.* To secure her son the succession to the throne, Queen Juana, a woman of virile strength and intrepid spirit, did all in her power to prejudice the king against Carlos de Viana, of whom the people were very fond; indeed, Juan, in compliance with the wish of the Catalonian cortes, intended to declare Don Carlos his successor. But Juana persuaded the king that the prince was conspiring against his life and

---

* *De Vita et Scriptis Eliæ Kapsali* . . . *acced. Excerpta ad Judeorum historiam pertinentia ex MS. Kapsalii Historia* [Padua, 1869], p. 58. The manuscript of Kapsali's chronicle is in the Ambrosiana in Milan.

crown, and that, by marrying Isabella of Castile, he intended to form a coalition with the latter's brother, Henry IV. Don Carlos was soon gotten rid of by poison, and an open revolt against the crown then broke out.

King Juan's most loyal adherents were the Jews, and they rendered him important services. For example, the skill of Abiatar Aben Crescas, his court physician and astrologer, restored his eyesight. The king exhibited so much liberality and good-will towards the Jews that his death caused them profound grief. Several Jewish communities of the kingdom assembled at Cervera to hold a memorial service; they sang Hebrew psalms and Spanish funeral songs, and Aben Crescas delivered a eulogy on the character of the good monarch.*

Juan's long-cherished hope to unite Aragon and Castile was virtually realized before he died. In 1469 his son Ferdinand married Isabella of Castile, Henry IV.'s sister, who, after the death of her brother Alfonso, had been recognized as his successor, and had been proclaimed ruler of Castile, though she did not really succeed to the throne until after the death of Henry IV. in 1474. The accomplishment of this marriage was materially promoted by Jews and Marranos, for it was as-

---

* Balaguer, *Historia de Cataluña*, lib. 17, cap. 27.

sumed that Ferdinand would, like his father, be
friendly towards the Jews, especially as he himself
had inherited Jewish blood from his mother. Don
Abraham Senior was particularly prominent in the
matrimonial negotiations. He was a rich Jew of
Segovia, who, owing to his sagacity, his eminent
services, and his position as the king's chief farmer
of taxes, exerted great influence. He urged the
grandees of Castile to support the proposed marriage between the Princess Isabella, who had many
suitors, and the distinguished Ferdinand of Aragon, who was already King of Sicily, and who,
even in his early youth, had displayed much valor.
Although Don Abraham met with violent opposition from a part of the Castilian nobility, he
induced the prince to make a secret journey to
Toledo. Isabella, who was favorably inclined
toward her cousin of Aragon, readily agreed to a
meeting. Ferdinand started on the journey without delay. Being destitute of means, he secured
a loan of twenty thousand sueldos from his "beloved servant," Jaime Ram, the son of a rabbi,
and one of the most distinguished jurists of his
time.* Ferdinand then crossed the frontier of

---

* In 1474 Ferdinand ordered his treasurer to repay the twenty
thousand sueldos to his "amado criado" Jaime Ram. The document, dated Caceres, March 10, 1474, is in the *Arch. de la Corona
de Aragon*, Reg. 3633, fol. 80 dorse.

Castile in disguise, and found shelter in the house of Abraham Senior, who took him quietly at night to the expectant princess.*

Pedro de la Caballeria, a very rich and distinguished young Marrano of Saragossa, a member of a family with many branches, was then entrusted with the task of winning over persons of rank who opposed the marriage project—Alfonso Carillo, the fickle Archbishop of Toledo, Pedro Gonzales de Mendoza, Bishop of Siguenza, who later became Cardinal of Spain, and others. By his power of persuasion, and by the extensive resources at his disposal, he, in fact, contrived that Ferdinand should be preferred to the King of Portugal, the Duke of Berri, the King of England, and all of Isabella's other suitors. Pedro de la Caballeria also had the distinguished honor of presenting to the royal bride, as Ferdinand's nuptial gift, a costly necklace valued at forty thousand ducats, and of paying the whole or a large part of its cost. The crown of Aragon was, in fact, so impoverished in those days that, on the death of King Juan, in 1479, jewels had to be taken from the treasury and sold, in order to bury him with such obsequies as were appropriate to royalty.†

---

* Kapsali, *op. cit.*, 60 sq.; Mariana, *De Rebus Hispaniæ*, lib. 24. cap. 1.

† Zurita, *Anales de Aragon*, iv. 165.

Abraham Senior, the intimate friend of the influential Andreas de Cabrera of Segovia, remained Isabella's most loyal adherent. He and Cabrera succeeded in effecting a reconciliation between her and her brother King Henry. Abraham stood so high in the esteem of the queen and the grandees that, in 1480, the cortes in Toledo, in recognition of his eminent services to the state, granted him a yearly stipend of ten thousand maravedis out of the revenues of the royal taxes.*

In Castile, as well as in Aragon, certain Jews, and especially many Marranos, wielded considerable influence. The name "Marrano" was applied to persons of Jewish stock whose parents or grandparents had been driven by despair and dire persecution to accept Christianity. The conversion was, however, only external, or feigned; at heart they adhered loyally to their ancestral religion. Though outwardly Christians, they secretly observed the tenets of the Jewish faith; this was not infrequently true even in the case of those who had become dignitaries of the Church. They celebrated the sabbath and holidays, assembled in subterranean or other secret synagogues, and practised Jewish rites in their homes. They thus remained Jews, and eventually they suf-

---

* *Colcccion de Documentos inéditos para la Historia de España,* xiii. 196.

fered torture and torments for their adhesion to Judaism.* The people and the rulers knew all this, but for a long time the Marranos were not molested, because, though they generally married within their own class, their family alliances extended into the highest strata of society. Their services were, moreover, regarded as indispensable. By their wealth, intelligence, and ability, they obtained the most important offices and positions of trust; they were employed in the cabinets of rulers, in the administration of the finances, in the higher law-courts, and in the cortes.

Though Ferdinand and Isabella were united by marriage, each had the guidance of a separate kingdom, so that they lived like two allied monarchs. They had not merely separate kingdoms, but also separate administrations and separate royal councils. The most important positions in these councils were held by Marranos—members of the families of De la Caballeria, Sanchez, Santangel, and others. Just as Luis de la Caballeria, the son of Don Bonafos, had been the confidant of King Juan of Aragon, so Jaime de la Caballeria, the brother of Luis, was the confidential friend of Ferdinand. Jaime accompanied him on his first journey to Naples, and constantly attended him with all the pomp of a prince. Alfonso, an-

---

* Kapsali, *op. cit.*, 56.

other brother of Luis, occupied the high position of Vice-Chancellor of Aragon, and Martin de la Caballeria was commander of the fleet at Mallorca. Luis Sanchez, a son of the rich Eleasar Usuf of Saragossa, was appointed president of the highest tribunal of Aragon; Gabriel Sanchez was chief treasurer, and his brother Alfonso was deputy-treasurer. Guillen Sanchez, Ferdinand's cup-bearer, was later promoted to the office of royal treasurer, and his brother Francisco was made steward of the royal household. Ferdinand also appointed Francisco Gurrea, Gabriel Sanchez's son-in-law, governor of Aragon. Whenever Ferdinand needed money he applied to the Santangels, who had commercial houses in Calatayud, Saragossa, and Valencia; of this family more will be said later. The Marranos Miguel de Almazan and Gaspar de Berrachina, the son of Abiatar Xamos, were the king's private secretaries.

In the cities, in the administration of public revenues, in the army, judiciary, and cortes, the Marranos, as has already been intimated, held important and influential offices. They were particularly prominent in Saragossa; this was the richest city of Aragon, owing to its extensive industries, which were largely conducted by Jews and Marranos. In Saragossa the Marrano Pedro Monfort was vicar-general of the archbishopric;

Juan Cabrero was archdeacon; and the priors of the cathedral were Dr. Lopez, a grandson of Mayer Pazagon of Calatayud, and Juan Artal, a grandson of Pedro de Almazan. One of the chief bailiffs of Saragossa was Pedro de la Cabra, a son of the Jew Nadassan Malmerca. Not less influential than in Aragon and at the Aragonese court were the Marranos who enjoyed the confidence of Queen Isabella. Her privy councillors and private secretaries were sons and grandsons of Jews; even her confessor, Hernando de Talavera, was the grandson of a Jewess.

The fact that the Marranos, whose number in the whole of Spain was very large, possessed great wealth and were everywhere esteemed for their intelligence, aroused envy and hatred. The fact that they also loyally adhered to their ancestral religion and had active intercourse with the Jews, disturbed the fanatic portion of the Spanish clergy. In 1478, the same year in which Muley Abul Hasan received the Spanish ambassador for the last time, in the most magnificent chamber of the Alhambra, and renounced the Spanish tribute, there assembled in Seville a number of clergymen, most of them Dominicans. Isabella was temporarily residing in that city, and she presided over the meeting. Its object was to determine what could be done to fortify and invigorate the Christian faith, especially among the Marranos. The clergy tried to convince the queen that the ordinary means of conversion, recommended by her, remained ineffective in the case of the New Christians, who did not believe in the fundamental doctrines of Christianity, but tenaciously clung to Judaism. Hence the assembly recommended the introduction of the Inquisition in the form in which it already existed in Sicily. Ferdinand, who in his boundless avarice and insatiable greed was always guided by considerations of self-interest and egoism, gladly accepted the proposition.

It has long been known, and Spanish historians of the present day freely admit, that the introduction of the Inquisition was due not so much to religious zeal as to material considerations; it was used as an instrument of avarice and of political absolutism. One aim of the power-loving king was to humble and subdue the Castilian nobles, who possessed great privileges, and among whom were not a few Marranos. His chief object was, however, to secure the wealth of the Marranos. A conflict with the Moors was inevitable; the signal of war had already been given. The royal treasury was empty. The people were already overburdened with taxes, and even the clergy were taxed, a thing that had never before happened in Spain. The king regarded the introduction of the

Inquisition, and the confiscation of the property of its victims, as the only available method of improving the desperate financial situation. Already in the cortes of 1465 certain extremists had proposed to prosecute the secret Jews, and to use their property in carrying on a war of extermination against the Moors. This project was executed fifteen years later by Ferdinand. As soon as the first tribunal of the Inquisition was established, Fernando Yaños de Lobon was ordered to transfer to the royal treasury the property of all condemned Jews.* The Inquisition enabled the king to satisfy his ambition fully. Just as Ferdinand, who was a dissembling bigot rather than a devout Christian, always talked religion, so he always commended peace, although he really desired to conquer the Moors, and to declare war against France after Louis XI.'s death. He, the ruler of a small kingdom, wished to become the head of a great state; the grandchild of the Toledan Jewess wrapped himself in the mantle of piety in order to elevate himself to the position of the most Catholic king.

The pious Isabella, who disliked to glorify religion at the expense of humanity, long opposed the

---

* "El Lic^{do} Fernand Yaños de Lobon, Adelantaide de Casa i Corte va comisiado para cobrar los bienes de los Judios que han seido e fueron condenados por los inquisidores." *Arch. de Sevilla, Libro de Cartas de* 1480, fol. 5, *Coleccion Muñoz* (Bibl. de la Academia de la Historia en Madrid).

introduction of the Inquisition, but she finally yielded to the exhortations of her exalted prelates and to the urgent solicitations of her husband. She was the pliant tool of spiritual advisers, who exercised unrestricted dominion over her, and virtually made her their slave. When, for example, she requested her confessor, Hernando de Talavera, who later became Archbishop of Granada, to allow her to confess either standing or sitting, he refused both alternatives, and insisted that she, the queen, should kneel at his feet. She yielded to his demand without a word of protest. It was entirely due to her that the Inquisition did not begin its horrible work until two years after permission for its establishment in Castile had been granted by the pope.

It is not our purpose to consider in detail the history of this institution with its cruel tortures, its scandalous procedure, and its thousands of victims. In composing such a history the pen must be dipped in blood and tears, and the writer should turn to account the great mass of unprinted material preserved in the state archives at Alcalá de Henares, most of which has never been utilized.*

---

* I intend, at no distant date, to write a history of the Spanish Inquisition, with special reference to the *Judaizantes*, or Judaizers, for which there is abundant material in the state archives of Alcalá de Henares, Seville, and elsewhere.

We have to examine merely the early operations of the Inquisition, and to call attention briefly to the victims belonging to those families whose members figure prominently in later chapters of this book.

The first tribunal was established at Seville. The first inquisitors entered that city in the beginning of January, 1481, and a few days later the first victims died at the stake. Several of the richest and most respected men of Seville were soon consigned to the flames—Diego de Suson, who possessed a fortune of ten million sueldos, and who had some repute as a Talmudist, Juan Abolafia, who had been for several years farmer of the royal customs, Manuel Sauli, and others. Several thousand persons, mainly rich Marranos, perished at the stake in Seville and Cadiz in 1481. Even the bones of those who had died long before were exhumed and burned, and the property of their heirs was ruthlessly confiscated by the state. Tribunals were soon established at Cordova, Jaen, and Ciudad-Real. The bull issued by Pope Sixtus IV., October 17, 1483, appointed the bloodthirsty Torquemada inquisitor-general, and allowed Ferdinand to extend the Inquisition to the hereditary lands of his house—Aragon, Catalonia, and Valencia. In this last province it had begun a year before, at the king's special command, to confiscate the property of the Marranos.* In the cities the introduction of the Holy Office met with violent opposition. The citizens of Teruel would not allow the inquisitors to perform their noxious work. When they approached Plasencia the members of the municipal council left the city. Barcelona feared that the new tribunal would be injurious to trade. The Aragonese, jealous of their old chartered rights, observed with profound dismay that the Inquisition was making their country dependent on Castile; they apprehended that this institution would cause the destruction of their ancient freedom.

In Aragon an arrangement for its introduction was made with the cortes, whose consent was necessary. The concurrence of that body was secured through the direct influence of Ferdinand and Isabella, both of whom had proceeded to Saragossa for that purpose. But scarcely had the two inquisitors, the Canon Pedro Arbués and the Dominican Gaspar Juglar, begun their work when they met with strong resistance. The opposition increased after the first *auto-de-fe*, and after proceedings had been begun against Leonardo or Samuel de Eli, one of the richest men of Saragossa.

---

* Pragmática de 12 Mai, 1482. *Libros de Credes e Ordinaciones* (*Arch. Municipal de Barcelona*).

Hence the states-general of the kingdom, having been summoned by Alfonso de la Caballeria, resolved to send a deputation to the king, which, in the name of the Marranos, offered him and the pope a considerable sum of money, on condition that the work of persecution and confiscation should be abandoned. But Ferdinand persisted in his determination, and the Inquisition continued its work with redoubled zeal.

In their despair the Marranos resorted to extreme measures. They determined to assassinate one of the inquisitors. A plan of action was formed in the house of Luis de Santangel, which still stands in the Mercado of Saragossa. The conspirators were Sancho de Paternoy, chief treasurer of Aragon, who had his own seat in the synagogue of Saragossa; Alfonso de la Caballeria, vice-chancellor of Aragon; Juan Pedro Sanchez, brother of Gabriel and Francisco Sanchez; Pedro de Almazan, Pedro Monfort, Juan de la Abadia, Mateo Ram, Garcia de Moros, Pedro de Vera, and other fellow-sufferers of Saragossa, Calatayud, and Barbastro. The plot was executed at the appointed time; on the night of September 15, 1485, Pedro Arbués was mortally wounded in the cathedral of La Seo, in Saragossa, by Juan de Esperandeu and Vidal Durango, the latter a Frenchman employed as a tanner by Esperandeu. Two days later Arbués died.* When the queen, who happened at that time to be in Cordova, heard of the murder of the inquisitor, she ordered that stringent proceedings should be instituted without mercy against all Marranos, not merely in Saragossa, but in every city of the land, and that their immense possessions should be confiscated by the state.†

Terrible punishment was inflicted on the conspirators. Juan de Esperandeu, a rich tanner, who owned many houses in the Calle del Coso (where the old Jewish bath for women still exists), was obliged to look on while his father, the tanner Salvador de Esperandeu, was burned at the stake. Juan himself, after his hands had been cut off, was dragged to the market-place on June 30, 1486, together with Vidal Durango, and quartered and burned. Juan de la Abadia, who had attempted suicide in prison, was drawn, quartered, and consigned to the flames. Mateo Ram's hands were chopped off, and he, too, died at the stake. Three months later the sisters of Juan de la Abadia, the knight Pedro Muñoz, and Pedro Monfort, vicar-general of the archbishopric of Saragossa, were

---

* Henry C. Lea, *The Martyrdom of S. Pedro Arbués* [*Papers of the American Hist. Assoc.*, vol. iii. New York, 1889.] The real murderer was Vidal, as is evident from a manuscript receipt preserved in the archives of the Cathedral of Saragossa.

† Pulgar, *Reyes Católicos* [Saragossa, 1567], fol. 184a.

burned as adherents of Judaism. Pedro's brother Jaime Monfort, deputy-treasurer of Catalonia, and his wife were burned in effigy in Barcelona.* The sentence of the chief treasurer, Sancho de Paternoy, was commuted to life imprisonment, at the request of his relative Gabriel Sanchez. In March and August, 1487, the notary Garcia de Moros, Juan Ram, son-in-law of Juan Pedro Sanchez, Juan de Santangel, and the knight Luis de Santangel died in the flames. The banker Juan Pedro Sanchez, the real head of the conspiracy, who had succeeded in escaping to Toulouse, was there recognized by the Aragonese students and arrested, but again secured his freedom. Gaspar de Santa Cruz, who had fled with him from Spain, died in Toulouse. Both were burned in effigy in Saragossa, also the other members of the Sanchez family—the merchant Bernard Sanchez, Brianda his wife, and Alfonso Sanchez, a man of letters; likewise the merchant Anton Perez, and Garcia Lopez. The wife of Lopez remained in Spain and died at the stake.†

The Inquisition spread terror and alarm every-

---

* *Coleccion de Documentos inéditos del Arch. General de la Corona de Aragon*, xxviii. 146.

† *Libro Verde de Aragon*, in Biblioteca Colombina, fol. 78 sq.; partly printed in *Revista de España*, xviii. 547-578; and in Amador de los Rios, *Historia de los Judíos*, iii. 616 sq. See also *Revue des Études Juives*, xi. 84 sq.

where. Thousands of Marranos suffered martyrdom for their religion. The more dreadfully they were persecuted, the greater became their love for their ancestral faith. Dalman de Tolosa openly declared that he, his mother, his brothers Gabriel and Luis, and their wives had, despite all hindrances, observed the Jewish law. A member of this family lived in Naples at the beginning of the sixteenth century, and was known as the *famoso mercador Catalan*. The wealthy Jacob of Casafranca, who had been deputy-treasurer of Catalonia, and whose mother died as a Jewess in the prison of the Inquisition, frankly confessed that the rabbi of Gerona had provided him with meat and all that he needed for the celebration of the Jewish holidays, and that in his house, in the Plaça de Trinidad of Barcelona, he had lived in accordance with the precepts of the Jewish religion and had read the law of Moses. The councillors of the Inquisition declared all his posterity to be Judaizers.*

Among those who were led to the great *auto-de-fe* at Tarragona, on July 18, 1489, clothed in the garb of penitents, were Andreas Colom, his wife

---

* " Jacobo de Casafranca, loctinent de thesover per lo Rey nostre Senyor en la Principat de Catalunya, habitador de la Ciutat de Barcelona, de linatge de Jueus," etc. *Coleccion de Documentos inéditos* . . . *de Aragon*, xxviii. 171, 188 sq.

Blancha, and his mother-in-law Francisca Colom. They all confessed that they had observed the rites, ceremonies, and holidays of the Jews.* What must have been the feelings of Christopher Columbus, or Colón,† when he heard that members of the Jewish race bore his name, and had been condemned by the Inquisition?

---

* "Nosaltres Andreu Colom franci Vilagut . . . tots del Archabisbat de Tarragona de nostra libera franquea agradable e spontanea voluntat abjuram renuntiam apartam e eunyam de nosaltret tota e en special aquesta de que som intamats e testificats la qual nosaltres havem confessada ço es de guardar e observar les ceremonies de la Ley de Moyses e fer los ritus e ceremonies e les solemnitats dels jueus les quals en special quiscu de nosaltres ha confessades les quals mes largament son contengendes en la sentencia que contra nosaltres ses donada e declarada." *Coleccion de Documentos inéditos* . . . *de Aragon*, xxviii. 37 sq.

† He was also called Colom. Winsor, *Columbus*, 157.

CHAPTER IV.

Columbus's First Appearance at the Spanish Court—The Junta of Cordova and the Conference at Salamanca—Abraham Zacuto—Isaac Abravanel.

THE ambitious plan which Ferdinand and Isabella energetically strove to realize was to establish a great kingdom, strengthened by political and religious unity. They desired, above all, to bring to an end the dominion of the Moors in Spain, and to expel the Mohammedans from the Peninsula.

When Columbus came to Spain, the war with the Moors had already begun. The systematic confiscation of the property of the "secret" Jews who had been condemned by the Inquisition brought enormous sums of money into the state treasury, and furnished Ferdinand and Isabella with means to continue the war. The victorious Spanish troops had already pressed forward and captured Zahara, Ronda, which had long been called "the Jews' town" (*de los Judios*), Setenil, and several other fortified cities.

It was after the close of the campaign of 1485 that the king and queen were first informed of

Columbus's presence in Spain, and of his project. They received this information from Luis de la Cerda, the brave Duke of Medina-Celi. Toward the close of that year he wrote from Rota to Isabella that he was sheltering in his palace a Genoese named Cristóbal Colón, who had come from Portugal, and who asserted that he could undoubtedly find a new ocean-route to India. The duke also wrote that he would gladly have placed the required ships at Columbus's disposal for the proposed voyage, and would have fitted out the expedition at his own expense, if it were not contrary to the law of the land, and contrary to the will of the queen. The duke was requested to induce the foreign projector to present himself before her.*

With letters of introduction from the duke to the queen and to Alonso de Quintanilla, the chief supervisor of the finances of Castile, Columbus proceeded to Cordova in January, 1486, and here, in May, he was accorded an audience with the Spanish rulers. In order to gain the favor of the pious queen, he wrapped himself in the mantle of

---

* The letter of the duke to the queen, and her answer, as well as the letter which Ferdinand and Isabella ordered Quintanilla to write to the duke, are no longer extant; they are known to us through the communication sent by the duke to Cardinal Mendoza, March 19, 1493.

religious fanaticism. He asserted that his undertaking was mainly in the interest of the Church; that he desired to disseminate Christianity in the newly discovered lands; and that, with the gold found in the ancient and much-renowned Ophir, the Holy Sepulchre could be wrested from the infidels. The confiding and fanatic Isabella listened to him with enthusiasm, and her soul was filled with joy in anticipation of making converts to Christianity. The king was actuated by wholly different motives. He had in mind the acquisition of territory rather than the dissemination of religion. He also took into account the cost of the enterprise and the dangers of failure, as well as the possible advantages. By nature distrustful, calculating, and suspicious, he was very reserved towards Columbus, who, in his shabby dress, had given the king the impression that he was an adventurer. Ferdinand thought that he must be all the more cautious because the Genoese had been repelled by the King of Portugal, the ruler of a state renowned above all for its maritime discoveries. Ferdinand and Isabella soon agreed that it was not an opportune time to accept the proposition made by Columbus. Like the King of Portugal, they determined to refer the plan for consideration to a learned commission. They named as its president the Prior of Prado, the noble Hernando de Talavera, who as confessor of the queen enjoyed her full confidence, and who, as archbishop of Granada, was afterwards so outrageously persecuted by the Inquisition.

This commission, which consisted of cosmographers and other eminent scholars, held several sittings, and to it Columbus submitted an exact plan of his enterprise, which he explained and interpreted. But either he failed to be explicit or the commissioners did not wish to understand him, for they reached the same conclusions as the Junta of Lisbon three years before; namely, that Columbus's assertions could not possibly be true, and that there were no unknown lands to be discovered. They strongly advised the king and queen not to venture into so vague an enterprise, for it would result in no advantage, but only in a loss of money and prestige.* Ferdinand, who in the midst of war could not find time carefully to examine Columbus's arguments, managed to induce the queen to put off the navigator with friendly words. Columbus was informed that while the war was pending such an important matter could not be settled, but that it should be considered as soon as peace was established.† This amounted to a rejection of the project. Columbus was

---

* Las Casas, *Historia de las Indias*, cap. 29.
† *Ibid.*, cap. 29; *Vida del Almirante*, cap. 11.

obliged, moreover, to endure the hatred and pungent derision of the courtiers and of all those who had heard of his plans. They all regarded him as a scheming adventurer, and in Cordova they derisively called him "The man with the cloak full of holes."

The unfavorable answer of Ferdinand and Isabella was a crushing blow not merely to Columbus, but also to his friends and patrons—to Alonso de Quintanilla, who had compassionately sheltered him for some time under his roof, and especially to Diego de Deza, a learned theologian of Jewish descent, whom Columbus himself reckons among his most influential patrons and supporters. Diego de Deza had a good reputation and was much esteemed. He had charge of the education of the heir-apparent, Prince Don Juan, and he was Bishop of Salamanca, as well as professor of theology at the university of that city, at that time the most celebrated seat of learning in the whole world. To diminish the force of the Junta's verdict he desired to refer Columbus's plan of discovery to eminent cosmographers and mathematicians for further examination. This he actually did without delay. He caused Columbus to come to Salamanca, and summoned to a conference the most distinguished professors of the university—mathematicians, astrologers, and cosmographers.

At its sessions, which were held at Valcuevo, near Salamanca, Columbus presented and defended his project.* Among others, there participated in this conference the astrologer Fray Antonio de Marchena, who always championed Columbus's cause, and the Jewish astrologer Abraham Zacuto, who, by his important contributions to his branch of knowledge, materially promoted Columbus's undertaking.

Abraham Zacuto, or Çacuto, was born in Salamanca about the year 1440, and was commonly called Zacuto of Salamanca.† His ancestors came from South France, and, as he himself informs us in his celebrated chronicle,‡ they remained steadfastly loyal to their religion in spite of all persecutions. He devoted himself to the study of mathematics, and especially astronomy, and won the favor of the Bishop of Salamanca, who allowed

---

* "El Illmo Sr. D. Fr. Diego de Deza, que fue obispo de esta ciudad . . . dio parto á los matematicos de esta celebre universidad. Hizoles juntas y retrados á la casa de estos PP. que tienen dos leguas de esta ciudad, llamado Valcuevo." Dorado, *Historia de la Ciudad de Salamanca* [Salamanca, 1776], 225.

Columbus was at Salamanca " á comunicar sus razones con los maestros de Astrologia y Cosmografia que leian estas facultades en la Universidad." Ant. Remesal, *Historia de Chiapa*, lib. 2, cap. 7. Concerning the Junta of Salamanca, see Tomas Rodriguez Pinilla, *Colon en España, Estud. hist. crít.* [Madrid, 1884].

† *Jochasin* (ed. Filipowski), 57^a.

‡ *Ibid.*, 223^a.

him to attend the university of that city. Here he became professor of astronomy,* and many Christian and Mohammedan disciples revered him as their teacher. His chief astronomical work was the *Almanach Perpetuum* with tables of the sun, moon, and stars, which, as his pupil Augustin Ricci informs us,† was prepared between 1473 and 1478, at the request of his patron, the bishop, to whom it was dedicated. It was translated from Hebrew into Latin and Spanish by his pupil Joseph Vecinho, or Vizino, and was printed at the press of Magister Samuel d'Ortas in Leiria. Owing to its wide circulation‡ it went through several editions during the author's lifetime.§

---

* The following is an extract from the dedication to the Bishop of Salamanca, prefixed to the *Almanach:* "Salmantini collegū alumnū me quantūcūque adesse voluisti, docturum videlicet quadruuiales facultates." Jachia confuses Saragossa with Salamanca when he asserts (*Schalschelet,* 50ᵃ) that Zacuto was also professor at Saragossa.

† "Abraham Zacuth, quem præceptorem in Astronomia habuimus in ciuitate Salamancha, jussu Episcopi tabulas astronomicas composuit." Ricci, *De motu octaviæ sphæræ* [Paris, 1521], p. 4.

‡ On page 222ᵃ of his *Jochasin,* writen in 1505, Zacuto rightly says: "My Tables are used in all Spain and also in the Orient."

§ This exceedingly rare book, which was first printed at Leiria in 1496, is entitled *Almanach perpetuum cuyas Radix est annum 1473 compositum ab excell. magistro in astronomia nomine bocrat Zacutus.* As far as I am aware, Abraham Zacuto is here for the first time called Bocrat. Was the Abraham Bocrat of

Columbus fully acknowledged the importance of Zacuto's contributions to science. He valued particularly Zacuto's *Almanach* and his *Tables*, with the improved quadrennial reckoning, the use of which was much simpler than any hitherto known, including even the *Ephemerides* of the German astronomer Johannes Müller, commonly called Regiomontanus. Zacuto's *Tables* always accompanied Columbus on his voyages, and rendered him

---

whom Abraham Gavison sings Abraham Zacuto? The work ends thus: "Expliciunt table tablarum astrorum Raby Abraham Zacuti astronome ser. regis emanuel Rex portugaliæ et cet. cum canonibus traductis a lingua ebrayca in latinum per magistrum Joseph vizinum discipulum ejus actoris." Then comes the title: "Tabule Tabularum celestium motuum astronomi Zacuti necnon stelarum fixarum longitudinem ac latitudinem ad motus vnitatem mira diligentia reducte ac in principio canones ordinatissime incipiunt felici sidere." Two tables follow. The next fifteen pages contain the *Canones en Romance* with the final words: "Aqui se acaba la recela de las tablas tresladadas del abrayco en latin e de latin en noestro vulgar romance por mestre jusepe vezino decipulo del actor de las tablas."

Columbus's copy of the work, with notes and glosses in his handwriting, is in the Colombina. See *Bibl. Colombina con notas bibl. del Dr. D. Simón de la Rosa y López* [Seville, 1888], i. 3.

The *Almanach Perpetuum*, "Joseph vecino traductor," was published in Venice, July 15, 1502, 4to. The *Tables*, revised by Alfonso de Corduba, appeared in Venice in 1496 and 1512, 4to, under the title *Tabulæ motuum cœlestium cum additamentis Alphonsis Hispani de Corduba*. There is a MS. Hebrew translation of the *Almanach* in the royal library at Munich. See M. Steinschneider, *Cat. Cod. MSS. Bibl. Reg. Monacensis* [Munich, 1875], p. 49.

inestimable service. To them, in fact, he and his crew once owed their lives. On his last voyage he had visited the coast of Veragua, the name of which is still perpetuated in the title of his present descendant, the Duke of Veragua. In its rich mines he found plenty of gold and precious stones. After leaving Veragua a terrible hurricane greatly injured his only two surviving caravels, rendering them unseaworthy. After he reached Jamaica he was in a desperate plight. The ungrateful Francisco de Porras had stirred up a conspiracy against him; Columbus himself was prostrated by illness; the natives were hostile to him and threatened his life; the few sailors who remained loyal to him were disheartened, and exhausted by hunger. The admiral and his followers anticipated certain death.

Thereupon he resorted to an expedient which is characteristic of him and of his time. By means of Zacuto's *Tables* he ascertained that there would be an eclipse of the moon on February 29, 1504. He then summoned certain caciques, or native chiefs, and told them that the God of the Spaniards was very angry with them because they did not give him and his sailors sufficient food, and that God would punish them by depriving them of the light of the moon, and by mercilessly subjecting them to the most pernicious influences. When night arrived, and the moon was invisible, the caciques and their followers raised a doleful wail, and, throwing themselves at the admiral's feet, they promised to provide him with plenty of provisions, and implored him to avert from them the impending evil. Columbus then retired on the pretence of communing with the Deity. When the thick darkness began to vanish, and the moon began to appear, he again came forth, and announced to the expectant caciques that their contrition had appeased the divine wrath. The full light of the moon soon beamed forth, and Columbus's object was attained; he encountered no more hostility, and obtained an abundance of food. "Thursday, February 29, 1504," says Columbus, "as I was in the Indies, on the Island of Jamaica, in the harbor of Sancta Gloria, situated about in the middle of the northern side of the island, there was an eclipse of the moon. As it began before the sun went down, I could note its termination only; the full light of the moon became visible exactly two and a half hours after nightfall. The difference in time between the Island of Jamaica in the Indies and the Island of Calis in Spain is seven hours and fifteen minutes, so that the sun sets in Calis seven hours and fifteen minutes earlier than in Jamaica." Columbus then refers to Zacuto's *Almanach*, the statement of which regarding the moon's eclipse exactly agrees with Columbus's observation.*

There can be no doubt that Zacuto, who made the personal acquaintance of Columbus in Salamanca, called the latter's attention to his treatises,† and that he also orally communicated to Columbus his theory concerning storms in the equinoctial regions—a theory which was of value to navigators. Zacuto, like his protector, Diego de Deza, was one of those who declared in favor of Columbus and his undertaking, and asserted that "the distant Indies, separated from us by great seas and vast tracts of land, can be reached, though the enterprise is hazardous."‡

The conference of Salamanca, in which Colum-

---

* "Jueves 29 de Febrero de 1504 estando yo en las yndias en la ysla de Janahica en el poerto que se diz de Sancta Gloria que es casi en el medio de la ysla, de la parte septentrional, obo eclipsis de la luna, y porque el comienco fue primero que el sol se pusiese non pude nótar saluo el termino de quando la luna acabo de volver en su claridad, y esto fue muy certificado dos oras y media pasadas de la noche. Cinco compolletas muy ciertas. La diferencia del medio de la ysla de Janahica en las yndias con la ysla de Calis en españa es siete oras y quinze minutos, de manera que en Calis se puso el sol primero que en Janahica con siete oras y quinze minutos de ora, vide Almanach." *Libro de las Profecias*, 59 sq.

† See above, p. 14.

‡ Gaspar Correa, *Lendas da India*, in *Collecção de Monumentos ineditos para a historia das Conquistas dos Portuguezes* [Lisbon, 1858], i. 10.

bus's resolute demeanor won the admiration of many and the sympathy of all, determined his fate, though its action was not of an official character, like that of the Junta of Cordova. The representations made by Diego de Deza and other learned men induced Ferdinand and Isabella to take Columbus into their service, and on May 5, 1487, they ordered the royal treasurer to deliver three thousand maravedis to the poor Genoese. Toward the end of August another sum of four thousand maravedis was assigned to him, with the express command to proceed to Malaga, which had been captured by the Spanish army a few weeks before. Here he became acquainted with the two most distinguished Jews of Spain, who were then at the king's court—the chief farmer of the taxes, Abraham Senior, of whom we have already spoken, and his friend Isaac Abravanel. They had undertaken to provision the royal armies, and by making great sacrifices they had done this to the special satisfaction of Queen Isabella. They were of extraordinary service to the kingdom, for they not merely devoted their own enormous fortunes to the purchase of arms and provisions, but they also induced other rich Jews to follow their example.*

---

* Amador de los Rios, *Historia de los Judíos de España y Portugal*, iii. 296 sq.

Don Isaac Abravanel belonged to an old and distinguished family. His grandfather, the "great" Samuel Abravanel, the richest and most influential Jew in Valencia, temporarily changed his religion in consequence of the great persecution of 1391, and called himself Alfonso Fernandez de Vilanova, after the name of one of his estates.* Samuel's son Judah Abravanel settled in Lisbon, and became treasurer of Prince Ferdinand, who, before his campaign against the Moors of Tangiers, made provision for the prompt payment of more than half a million reis which he had borrowed from Don Judah. Isaac Abravanel enjoyed the complete confidence of King Affonso V. of Portugal, and was on the most friendly terms with the members of the house of Braganza. But after Affonso's death he was obliged to resort to flight, as he was a friend of the powerful Duke of Braganza, whom King João II. had condemned to death. He went to Castile and soon won the favor of the king and queen.† It is possible that

---

* "E hir lo gran don Samuel Abravalla se batejá ab gran solemnitat en lo real d'En Gastó, sots padrinatge del marqués, é ha nom Alfonso Fernandez de Vilanova, per un loch, que éll ha en lo marquesat, apelat Vilanova." *Carta de los Jurados de Valencia*, in Amador de los Rios, *Historia de los Judíos*, ii. 603. According to Zacuto (*Jochasin*, 224) he called himself Juan de Sevilla.

† Concerning Isaac Abravanel's life and works, see Kayserling, *Geschichte der Juden in Portugal*, 72 sq.

Columbus, during his residence in the capital of Portugal, had already made the acquaintance of this honored and accomplished man. Isaac Abravanel was one of the first to render financial assistance to Columbus's undertaking.

CHAPTER V.

COLUMBUS IN SANTA FÉ—THE FALL OF GRANADA—THE POSITION OF THE SANTANGELS; THEIR PERSECUTION BY THE INQUISITION—LUIS DE SANTANGEL'S INTERPOSITION IN FAVOR OF COLUMBUS—THE QUEEN'S JEWELS, AND SANTANGEL'S LOAN FOR THE EQUIPMENT OF THE EXPEDITION.

WE do not know why Columbus was called to Malaga or how long he stayed there. He soon returned to Cordova, where he became intimate with Beatrice Enriquez, a poor girl, who has been erroneously called the daughter of a Jew. He was soon neglected again by the king and queen, who gradually ceased to grant him subsidies. He lived in the greatest poverty with his mistress Beatrice, by whom he had a son. Tired of prolonged delays, he resumed the negotiations with the King of Portugal which had been discontinued several years before; but these new overtures were also unsuccessful, and he now determined to lay his project before the King of France.

He first proceeded to the monastery of La Rábida near Palos, either to see his son Diego before leaving Spain, or, more probably, to inform his patron, the Prior Juan Perez de Marchena, of his plans and to bid him farewell. At the gate of this monastery, which was situated on an eminence, he had knocked as a poor pilgrim on his arrival in Spain, and had begged for bread and water for his little son. The prior, who was considerably interested in Columbus's plans, did all in his power to prevent the proposed departure from Spain, and he was seconded in his efforts by Garcia Fernandez, the physician of Palos.* Marchena, who had been the queen's confessor, and was highly esteemed by her as a good astrologer, wrote an urgent letter to Isabella, recommending the Genoese and his undertaking in the warmest terms. This letter was carried to the queen, who was then at Santa Fé, by Sebastian Rodriguez, a mariner of Lepe. The neighboring city of Granada had already been forced to capitulate. In this splendid Moorish town a revolt had just broken out among the Moslems, but they had been somewhat pacified by Ferdinand's promise that all Moors and Jews should enjoy religious freedom, and that they might depart without hindrance.†

---

* Dr. Calatraveño, *Hechos médicos relacionados con el descubrimiento de América* [Madrid, 1892].

† The original manuscript of the capitulation of Granada (in the Escurial, MS. 7 del siglo xv.) has the following: "Otrosi suplicamos a vuestras Altezas manden dar sus cartas de seguro

After deliberating with the king, Isabella wrote at once to the prior that he should come as soon as possible to the royal camp, and bring with him Columbus, who was still in the monastery, awaiting an answer. She also sent two thousand maravedis in order that the navigator might appear before their majesties decently clothed. In company with the prior he then started for Santa Fé, and arrived there, in the midst of the tumult of war, in December, 1491, shortly before the crescent disappeared from the western tower of the Alhambra. In Santa Fé he found his most influential patron, Pedro Gonzales de Mendoza, the primate, or, as he is called by Peter Martyr,* "the third king of Spain," who presided over a meeting of distinguished men summoned to examine the project of discovery. Columbus boldly advocated his scheme, and soon convinced the primate that his assertions were true. It was not difficult for the latter to induce the queen to give her approval to the plan of exploration.

After a seven years' conflict, comparable only with the Trojan war, Granada fell into the power

---

para los Judios, y licencia para levar lo suyo, e que si sin culpa de alguno por no haber navio alguno quedaren en la costa que haya termino para se partir." In the margin are the words: "Que se haya."

* Pedro Martyr, *Epistolæ*, lib. 8, epist. 159.

of Spain. On Friday, January 2, 1492, the Spanish standard first floated from the highest tower of the old Moorish palace, and the two sovereigns ceremoniously entered the conquered Moorish capital. On the same day Ferdinand announced to all the cities of his kingdom that, after many great conflicts which had cost much noble blood, it had pleased God to allow the Christian armies to vanquish the Moors. Since the conquest of Granada papal gratitude has permitted the ruler of Spain to bear the title His Most Catholic Majesty.

In all the cities of Spain the fall of the Moorish dominion and the triumph of the Christian religion were celebrated with songs of rejoicing. The Jews went about in sorrow and with bowed heads, for the conquest of the Moslem also decided their fate, in spite of the important part which they had played in securing the victory; from the palace of the Alhambra the Catholic king and queen soon issued the cruel edict of their expulsion. At the pompous spectacle of the entry of the Christian armies into Granada there were present two men of extraordinary importance, two wholly dissimilar men, with whose acts Spain's later greatness as well as her downfall, her whole distracted destiny, was closely connected—a proud priest and a morose beggar.

The priest was Cardinal Ximenez de los Cisneros, the very learned grand inquisitor, who wished to turn all Moors and Jews into Christians, and who persecuted the Marranos with the utmost rigor. The beggar was Christopher Columbus, with whom the two sovereigns now began to negotiate in earnest. Within reach of the object of his long-cherished hopes and desires, Columbus was impelled by his ambition and insatiable avarice to make enormous demands; he wished to be appointed admiral, viceroy, and governor for life over all lands which he might discover. Ferdinand was not inclined to grant such demands or to concede such far-reaching privileges. Hence the negotiations with Columbus were suspended, and in January, 1492, he left Granada with the definite purpose of going to the French court.

Then, when his cause seemed to be lost, several persons resolutely interposed in his favor; they were Juan Cabrero, Luis de Santangel, Gabriel Sanchez, and Alfonso de la Caballeria, all men of Jewish extraction. When Luis de Santangel heard that the negotiations with Columbus had been definitely broken off, he felt as much sorrow and distress as if he himself had been afflicted with some great misfortune.*

Let us pause to inquire who Luis de Santangel

---

* Las Casas, *Historia de las Indias*, cap. 32.

was. In the fifteenth and sixteenth centuries the family of Santangel or Sancto Angelo was one of the richest, most influential, and most powerful in Aragon. When, in consequence of great persecutions and of the Jew-baiting sermons of Vicente Ferrer, many Jews in Calatayud, Daroca, Fraga, Barbastro, and other cities changed their religion in order to save their lives, the Santangels also adopted Christianity. Like the Villanuevas, whose ancestor was Moses Patagon,* and the Clementes, who were descended from Moses Chamorro, the Santangels also emanated from Calatayud, the ancient Calat-al-yehud, which in the fourteenth century had one of the richest Jewish communities in Aragon. The ancestor of the Santangels is said to have been the learned Azarias Ginillo, whose wife could not be induced to forsake Judaism, even outwardly. A few years later, however, she married Bonafos de la Caballeria, and, together with her husband, she followed the example of Azarias and became a Christian. Azarias Ginillo, or Luis de Santangel, as he called himself, was an eminent jurist. He had several sons and daughters. One of these, together

---

* Also called Pazagon. Members of this family also resided in Portugal. Isaac Pazagon was president of the Jewish community in Coimbra about the year 1360. See Kayserling, *Geschichte der Juden in Portugal*, 24.

with her lover, a certain Marzilla, was murdered by her husband. The other daughter married Pedro Gurrea, a secret Jew, and their son Gaspar wedded Anna de la Caballeria, a secret Jewess.* Azarias's sons, Alfonso—who, like his father, studied law—Juan Martin, and Pedro Martin, lived in Daroca, and secured protection and privileges from King Ferdinand I. of Aragon.†

Azarias-Luis de Santangel was not only learned, but also prosperous, though not wealthy. In the year 1459 his grandsons, the jurist Luis de Santangel, junior, and Leonardo de Santangel of Calatayud, petitioned King Juan of Aragon to allow them to dig for gold and silver coins and other treasures which had been buried by their parents and grandparents. They proposed to dig beneath the houses which, as orphans of tender age, they had inherited from their parents, but which they had afterwards sold to the Jew Abraham Patagon or to his brother Raymundo Lopez. The property adjoined the estates of Fernando Lupo and Luis Sanchez in the Villanueva quarter of Calatayud. Luis de Santangel offered to give to the state treasury one-fifth of all that he might find. The king granted their petition on October 24, 1459, on condition that they should undertake the excava-

---

* *Revista de España*, xviii. 249 sq.   † Appendix i.

tions at their own expense, and with the consent of Abraham Patagon, the present owner of the houses, and that these houses should be restored to the condition in which they were found.*

In consequence of their keen intellects, their activity, and their wealth, the Santangels secured great influence and high positions of trust; they were prominent jurists and teachers of law, and occupied important posts in the cortes, in the municipalities, in the administration of the state, and in the Church.

Azarias-Luis de Santangel, who had the reputation of being an excellent lawyer,† attained the position of Zalmedina, or Zavalmedina, a name given to the judge in ordinary of the capital, who was appointed by the king.‡ To escape persecution and to demonstrate his Christian faith, he devoted his son Pedro Martin to the ministry, and the latter became Bishop of Mallorca as well as adviser of King Juan II. Pedro Martin left a legacy to provide for the marriage of poor orphan girls of his family, and by the terms of his will the trust was to be administered by the city of

---

* Appendix ii.

† Zurita, *Anales de la Corona de Aragon*. vol. iv., lib. 16, cap. 25.

‡ Zalmedina is an abbreviation of Zavalmedina, which is derived from an Arabic word meaning "lord," and from *medina*, "city." *Coleccion de Documentos inéditos de Aragon*, viii. 115.

Barbastro.* Another Martin de Santangel, the bishop's nephew, became provincial of Aragon, and resided in Saragossa. Another Luis de Santangel, acting as ambassador of King Alfonso V. of Aragon, negotiated with the Sultan of Babylonia concerning a commercial treaty. The most far-reaching influence was attained by those members of the family who had houses and property in Daroca, Barbastro, Teruel, Alcañiz, and in other towns of Aragon and Valencia, especially in Calatayud, Valencia, and Saragossa.

The lawyer Luis de Santangel, the one who had sought for the treasures buried by his parents in Calatayud, held the high office of treasury advocate (*fisci advocatus*). The names of Luis de Santangel and Luis de la Caballeria, the treasurer-general, were subscribed to a patent of nobility and grant of privileges issued on December 4, 1461, in Calatayud, by King Juan of Aragon, to his "well-beloved" soldier Juan Gilbert and his descendants.† At a meeting of the cortes of

---

* "Concordia entre la ciudad de Barbastro y Pedro Lunel y su Muger D. Maria de Santangel sobre el legado de Pedro de Santangel para casar pupilas. . . . Es patrona de este legado la ciudad segun la clausula que se incerta en el testamento del dicho Pedro de Santangel. Llama descendientes pobres de su linaje y el legado de 513 livres." (1473.) *Archivo de Zaragoza.*

† The original document, which was formerly in the archives of Calatayud, is now in the state archives at Alcalá de Henares.

Aragon in the year 1473, this Luis de Santangel represented the knights and nobles, while in the same year Antonio de Santangel of Calatayud represented that city.* The latter interposed on behalf of the Jewish community of Hijar a few days after the expulsion of the Jews from Spain.†

In the middle of the fifteenth century the Santangels of Valencia and Saragossa were the Rothschilds of their time. At the head of the Valencian house was the merchant Luis de Santangel the elder. In the year 1450 Luis already gained the favor of King Alfonso V. of Aragon;‡ he also had uninterrupted intercourse with King Juan II. He was farmer of the *de la Mata* salt-works near Valencia, for which, according to a contract of July 9, 1472, he had to pay a yearly rent of 21,100 sueldos to the Marrano Juan de Ribasaltas; §

---

* Miguel Mir, *Influencia de los Aragoneses en el descubrimiento de América* [Palma de Mallorca, 1892], pp. 29 sq.; Eduardo Ibarra y Rodríguez, *D. Fernando el Católico y el descubrimiento de América* [Madrid, 1892], pp. 191 sq.

† "Anton de Santangel, habitante en Calatayud, reclama una cuenta sobre la aljama de Judios en Hijar." Borja, Aug. 10, 1492. *Arch. de la Corona de Aragon*, Reg. 3650, fol. 109.

‡ Documents dated Perpignan, March 18 and July 8, 1450. *Arch. de la Corona de Aragon*, Reg. 3253, fol. 132, and Reg. 3254, fol. 58 sq.

§ " . . . valeamus arrendare et titulo arrendamenti concedere vobis delecto et fideli nostro Ludouico de Santoangelo mercatori ciuitatis Valentie natu majori salinas vulgo dictas de

he was also farmer of the royal domains and customs.* After the death of Luis the elder in 1476, his wife Brianda† assumed the management of his business, and his son Luis de Santangel the younger, who was a royal councillor in Valencia, became farmer of the royal domains,‡ while the farming of the salt-works, after the termination of the elder Luis's contract, passed to his relative and partner Jaime de Santangel.§ Jaime's coffers

---

la mata per set anys," etc. Document dated Ajatero, July 9, 1472. *Arch. de la Corona de Aragon*, Reg. 3641, fol. 26. Beatrice de Ribasaltas, wife of Juan de la Caballeria, was subjected to public penance on July 17, 1491.

* " Orden al mercador de Valencia Luis de Santangel mayor de edad para que de lo que ha de dar al Rey por varon del ordenamiento de peage y otros seruicios pague á Jaime de Santangel criado y copero del Rey 1183 sueldos y seis dineros moned. barcel." Document dated Barcelona, December 28, 1473. *Arch. de la Corona de Aragon*, Reg. 3641, fol. 35.

"Confirmacion del nombramiento de recepcion en las rentas reales de Valencia que á favor de Luis de Santangel mercader en dicha ciudad hizo D. Juan en Barcelona, 16 Agosto, 1475." Burgos, September 9, 1475. There is a confirmation dated Caceres, May 26, 1478. *Arch. de la Corona de Aragon*, Reg. 3519, fol. 58, and Reg. 3633, fol. 91.

† " Causam vertentem propter Briandam de Sanctangel viduam Ludouici et Jacobum de Sanctangel eorumque filios tam ut heredes patris eorum." *Ibid.*, Reg. 3633, fol. 9.

‡ The contract is dated Madrigal, April 8, 1476. *Ibid.*, Reg. 3633, fol. 18. See also Reg. 3547, fol. 127 sq.: "Luis de Sanctangel consejero ciudadano de Valencia."

§ " Concordia entre el Rey y el magnífico Jaime de Santangel escribano de racion y consejero de Su Majestad sobre las salinas

were always open to Juan II., who appointed him royal cup-bearer, and they were also open to Ferdinand, his son and successor. Jaime lent the latter large sums of money to subdue the rebellious Catalonians, to recover the county of Rousillon from the King of France, to whom it had been pledged, and to conquer Granada.* Whenever Ferdinand needed money he appealed to his friends the Santangels in Valencia, and never in vain.

To this family which stood in such high repute in all Aragon, Catalonia, and Valencia, the Inquisition proved fatal. As we have already seen, the introduction of the Holy Office was opposed by the richest and most distinguished Marranos of Saragossa. The Santangels were among those who, at heart true to their old faith, headed the conspiracy against the Inquisitor Pedro d'Arbués. As the spot where Arbués received his death-blow

---

de la mata de Valencia." Victoria, December 29, 1484. *Arch. de la Corona de Aragon*, Reg. 3641, fol. 2.

* " El Rey conceso á su copero Jacobo de Sanctangelo treze mil sueldos de moneda barcel. en pago de los consilios que al monarca habia prestado en la guerra para reclamar á la obediencia al Principal de Cataluña." Barcelona, October 30, 1473. *Ibid.*, Reg. 3461, fol. 44. He aided the king with the same sum " en la reduccion de Rossillon que adhuc sub obediencia regis detinetur." *Ibid.*, Reg. 3519, fol. 173. For the loan "in hoc bello quod contra Granatam gerimus," see the document dated Cordova, September 1, 1485. *Ibid.*, Reg. 3641, fol. 105.

is still pointed out in the metropolitan church of La Seo, so too one may still see in the large and beautiful market-place, or Mercado, of Saragossa the stately houses which in the flourishing days of the Aragonese capital belonged to Luis and Juan de Santangel.* The Santangels were also among the first Jewish heretics to mount the funeral pile. The first victim of the Inquisition in Saragossa was Martin de Santangel, who was burned July 28, 1486; eleven months later, August 18, 1487, Mosen Luis de Santangel, father-in-law of the treasurer Gabriel Sanchez, met the same fate. On July 10, 1489, the mother of Gabriel Gonçalo de Santangel, and six years later Gabriel himself, died at the stake. The lawyer Juan de Santangel and his brother Luis, who both resorted to timely flight and reached Bordeaux in safety, were burned in effigy, the one on March 17, 1487, the other on June 1, 1492; all their property, real and personal, was confiscated by the state. Juan was exiled forever from Spain, and his three daughters, Louisa, Agnes and Laura, who had been reared in affluence, were reduced to extreme

---

* In the year 1512 Juan Sanchez de Romeral, " procurador sindico de los Jurados de Zaragoza," grants a licence for the repair of the façade of a house adjoining " con casas de Micer Luis de Santangel, y con casas de los herederos de Juan de Albacer é con el mercado." *Arch. del ayuntamiento de Zaragoza.*

poverty. Even the hard-hearted Ferdinand was moved at this spectacle; as a special token of royal grace and in recognition of their father's services, he granted them, on January 19, 1488, a yearly pension of 1,500 sueldos out of the taxes of the Jewish community in Jaca.* We do not know whether this annuity came to an end with the expulsion of the Jews and the cessation of their taxes.

Snares were constantly laid by the Holy Office to entrap the members of the Santangel family and to secure their property. Jaime Martin was burned on March 20, 1488; Donosa de Santangel six months later; Simon de Santangel and his wife Clara Lunel, betrayed by their own son, were burned in Lerida on July 30, 1490.† In order to have a quasi-legal pretext for confiscating their property for the use of the state, Violante de Santangel, ‡ the wife of Alfonso Gomez of Huesca, and Gabriel de Santangel of Barbastro were condemned, and their remains were exhumed and publicly burned. Gabriel's estates were sold by the king to Miguel Vivo, Abbot of Aljoro, for

---

* See Appendix iii.

† *Revue des Études Juives*, xi. 87.

‡ " Violante de Santangel, muger de Alfonso Gomez en Huesca, condemnata et ejus ossa exhumata et igni tradita, sus bienes á la Curia." Granada, September 20, 1491. *Arch. de la Corona de Aragon*, Reg. 3649, fol. 18.

18,000 sueldos.* All the members of the family who escaped with their lives were at least pilloried as Jews or Jewish heretics. Thus the jurist Pedro de Santangel, Juan Thomas and Miguel de Santangel,† the wife of Lopez-Patagon, and Lucretia de Santangel, all had to go in public procession clothed as penitents and solemnly swear never again to practise Jewish rites. The Inquisition carried on, in fact, a veritable war of destruction against all the members of this family; without regard to age, sex, or position, they were consigned to the flames or obliged to do public penance, and that, too, even as late as the sixteenth century. ‡

On July 17, 1491, Luis de Santangel also appeared in a variegated *sambenito* as an adherent of Judaism. He stands in the foreground of the event of that time which figures so prominently in the world's annals; impartial historians must

---

* " Gabriel de Santangel de Barbastro condemnatus et ejus ossa exhumata et igni tradita, sus bienes á la Curia, y despues el Rey los venden á D. Miguel Viuo abad de Aljoro á cambio de 18,000 sueldos." Granada, May 12, 1492. *Ibid.*, Reg. 3650, fol. 44.

† Miguel was an alderman of Saragossa.

‡ The following were burned : Isabel de Santangel, October 4, 1495 ; Fernando de Santangel of Barbastro, October 19, 1496 ; Juana de Santangel, wife of Pedro de Santa Fé, September 13, 1499. A Luis de Santangel of Calatayud did public penance on June 10, 1493, and another Luis de Santangel on October 19, 1496. See *El Libro Verde*, in *Revista de España*, vol. xviii.

unhesitatingly assign to him an important rôle in the discovery of America.

He was the son of the rich Luis de Santangel who was the farmer of the royal taxes and customs in Valencia, an office which he himself subsequently held; he was the nephew of the Luis de Santangel who died at the stake in Saragossa. King Ferdinand appointed him *escribano de racion*, chancellor of the royal household in Aragon. He also held the same influential position of *contador mayor*, or comptroller-general, in Aragon which was occupied by Alonso de Quintanilla in Castile. He was a favorite of King Ferdinand, enjoyed the latter's complete confidence, knew all his secrets, and transacted all kinds of business for him. The king held him in high esteem for his fidelity, his sagacity, his extraordinary industry and administrative talent, his sterling integrity and his complete devotion to the crown; whenever Ferdinand wrote to him, he called him "the good Aragonese, excellent, well-beloved councillor." * On the other hand, Luis de Santangel owed his royal friend not only his eminent position but also his life; had it not been for the

---

* " . . . . en atencion á sus meritos, fides, solertia, industria, sufficientia, disposicione et animi probitate." *Arch. de la Corona de Aragon*, Reg. 3616, fol. 169 sq., 208, etc. See also Victor Balaguer, *Cristóbal Colón* [Madrid, 1892], p. 43.

king's direct intervention, he and his children would have shared the fate of his uncle and that of many of his relatives.

Luis de Santangel was the Beaconsfield of Spain. Like that English statesman—who was of Jewish stock and whose ancestors were also persecuted by the Inquisition and driven from Spain—Luis was characterised at once by particularism and universalism, enthusiasm and sagacity, subjective patriotism and objective devotion to other nationalities. He was a good Aragonese, and yet he worked for the unity of Spain; he was ardently devoted to his country, and he carefully considered the advantages which it would derive from maritime discoveries. As the head of a great mercantile house in Valencia and as farmer of the royal customs, he had intercourse with Genoese merchants long before Columbus came to Spain. Already in 1479 he was commissioned by Ferdinand to settle a disputed question in which some Genoese mariners in Valencia were concerned; the dispute was regarding certain customs-duties. At the same time he was also ordered to pay for the cloth imported from Lombardy for the use of the royal household.*

---

* The document is dated Trugillo, February 6, 1479. *Arch. de la Corona de Aragon*, Reg. 3633, fol. 90; see also Reg. 3633, fol. 70.

Probably Columbus was introduced to the merchant of Valencia by some of his countrymen, and may have early made Santangel's acquaintance.

Luis de Santangel became the leader of the Aragonese who at the last moment successfully interposed on behalf of Columbus. He was actively assisted by the royal chamberlain Juan Cabrero, the son of Martin Cabrero and Isabel de Paternoy, who were both of Jewish lineage and whose kinsmen were victims of the Inquisition.* Juan was the confidential friend and constant companion of Ferdinand the Catholic; he fought at the king's side in the Moorish wars, and was his faithful adviser in all affairs of state; he enjoyed Ferdinand's confidence to such an extent that he was made the executor of the king's will.

As soon as Santangel heard of Columbus's departure and the termination of his negotiations, he went to the queen, if not at Ferdinand's request, at least with his consent, and earnestly expressed his surprise that so magnanimous a patron of great enterprises had not the courage to enter on an undertaking from which she could reasonably anticipate enormous wealth, great increase of territory, and immortal glory both for

---

* Juan de Paternoy's remains were burned as those of a Jewish heretic, at the *auto-de-fe* in Saragossa on June 20, 1497.

the crown and for the Church. He represented to her that the amount of money demanded for the enterprise was comparatively small, and that the remuneration which the explorer demanded for such discoveries as he might make, should not occasion much hesitation. Columbus himself, Santangel went on to say, undertook to bear a part of the expense, and ventured his honor, nay even his life. In all probability the Genoese was a wise and sagacious man, well qualified to achieve success. Many eminent scholars to whom the queen had submitted his project for examination had approved of it, and Columbus's opponents could advance no valid arguments against his contentions. If, as Columbus predicted, some other European power should have the good fortune to act as his patron and to reap the fruits of these discoveries, the kingdom of Spain, its rulers, and the whole nation would suffer much shame and detriment. If the queen did not seize this opportunity, she would reproach herself all her life; her enemies would deride her, and her descendants would blame her; she would impair her honor and the renown of her royal name; she would injure her states and the welfare of her subjects.*

These arguments of Santangel produced a pro-

---

* Las Casas, *Historia de las Indias*, cap. 32.

found impression upon the queen. She thanked him for his advice, and promised him her consent to the undertaking; but she desired to wait awhile until the kingdom recovered its strength, for its financial resources had been exhausted by the recent, long-continued war. It is said that she even promised to pledge her jewels to secure money for the equipment of the armada, if Columbus could not brook further delay in the execution of his enterprise.* Santangel, the story continues, was much delighted at the queen's resolve, and declared that it was not necessary for her to pledge her jewels; he would be pleased, he said, to advance the money necessary for the expedition, and would be glad of the opportunity to perform so small a service for her and for his master the king.† This story, invented to glorify Queen Isabella, has recently been relegated to the realm of fable.‡ The sale of crowns and jewels by Spanish rulers was not, however, a rare occurrence.

---

* "Mas prestándole Luis de Santangel diez y seis mil Ducados sobre sus joyas." Pizarro y Orellano, *Varones ilustres del Nuevo Mundo* [Madrid, 1639], p. 10. This assertion is accepted by Prescott in his *History of Ferdinand and Isabella*, and by Washington Irving in his excellent *Life of Columbus*.

† Las Casas, *Historia de las Indias*, cap. 32 ; Muñoz, *Historia del Nuevo Mundo*, vol. ii., cap. 31.

‡ See the excellent essay of the learned academician Cesáreo Fernández Duro, *Las joyas de Isabel la Católica*, in his *Tradiciones infundadas* [Madrid, 1888].

Doña Sancha, wife of Ferdinand I. the Great of Castile, sold her jewels in order to pay the soldiers for their services in the war against the Moors. When Alfonso X. the Wise of Castile, desired to put down the rebellion of the Infante Don Sancho, he borrowed a large sum of money from the Moor Jacob Abd-el-Hacer, and gave him the crown jewels as security. In order to carry on the siege of Algeciras in 1344, Alfonso XI. was compelled to pawn his crown; and in the expedition against Naples Alfonso V. of Aragon pledged his crown and his table-plate for two hundred and eighty-seven ducats.*

At that time neither Aragon nor Castile, neither Ferdinand nor Isabella, had at their disposal enough money to equip a fleet. Santangel, who was always ready to oblige the crown, advanced seventeen thousand florins—nearly five million maravedis.† The queen's jewels were not de-

---

* P. Fidel Fita, *Boletín de la real Academia de la Historia*, xii. 213.

† "Y porque auia necesidad de dineros para su expedicion, á causa de la guerra, los prestó para fazer la primera armada de las Indias y su descubrimiento el escribano de racion luys de Sant Angel;" Gonçalo Fernandez de Oviedo, *Coronica de las Indias* [1547], p. 5ᵇ. "Hallandose los Reyes en necesidad de dineros para esta empresa, prestó les diez y seys mil Ducados Luys de Sant Angel, su escribano de raciones;" Garibay, *Compendio historial de las Chronicas de todos los Reynos d'España* [Antwerp, 1571], lib. 19, cap. 1, p. 1371. "Y por que los Reyes no tenian

manded as security; all of them were not, in fact, in her possession at that time, for she had pledged her necklace during the late war. Owing to the jealousy which still exists even at the present day between Castile and Aragon, Aragonese writers* have recently discussed the question whether Luis de Santangel lent this money out of his own pocket or whether he secured it indirectly from the state treasury through Gabriel Sanchez, the treasurer-general of Aragon. Apart from the fact that the treasury of Aragon as well as that of Castile was empty in consequence of the long war with the Moors,† Santangel's extraordinary services in this matter are clearly demonstrated by the excessive praise which Ferdinand accorded his "well-beloved" Luis de Santangel, and by the many proofs of gratitude which the

---

dineros para despacher á Colon, les prestó Luys de Sant Angel, su escribano de racion, seis cuentos de maravedis, que son en cuenta mas gruesa 16,000 ducados;" Gómara, *Historia de las Indias*, cap. 15, p. 167. "Y para el gasto de la Armada prestó Luis de Santangel escribano de raciones de Aragon diez y siete mil florines;" Bart. Leonardo de Argensola, *Anales*, lib. I, cap. 10.

* Eduardo Ibarra y Rodriguez, *D. Fernando el Católico y el descubrimiento de América* [Madrid, 1892], pp. 164 sq.

† Felipe de la Caballeria of Saragossa had lent 9,022 sueldos to Ferdinand's father, King Juan of Aragon, who died in January, 1479. It was not until 1493 that Gabriel Sanchez was ordered by the king to pay this debt. Document dated Barcelona, August 30, 1493. *Arch. de la Corona de Aragon*, Reg. 3616, fol. 182.

king gave him.* Of these we shall have more to say later.

That he advanced this money out of his own pocket is proved beyond question by the original account-books, which were formerly in the archives of Simancas and which are still preserved in the *Archivo de Indias* in Seville. In the account-book of Luis de Santangel and the treasurer Francisco Pinelo, extending from 1491 to 1493, Santangel is credited with an item of 1,140,000 maravedis which he gave to the Bishop of Avila † for Columbus's expedition. In another account-book, that of Garcia Martinez and Pedro de Montemayor, there is the following item: Alonso de las Cabezas, treasurer of war in the bishopric of Badajoz, by order of the Archbishop of Granada, dated May 5, 1492, paid to Alonso de Angulo for Luis de Santangel, the king's *escribano de racion*, whose authorization was presented with the aforesaid order, 2,640,000 maravedis, to wit, 1,500,000 in payment to Isaac Abravanel of money which he had lent their majesties in the Moorish war, and the remaining 1,140,000 maravedis in payment to

---

* See Appendix v. and vi.; also the document dated Barcelona, May 20, 1493, in *Arch. de la Corona de Aragon*, Reg. 3616, fol. 169 dorse.

† This Bishop of Avila afterwards became Archbishop of Granada.

the aforesaid *escribano de racion* of money which he advanced to equip the caravels ordered by their majesties for the expedition to the Indies and to pay Christopher Columbus, the admiral of that fleet.* On May 20, 1493, on which day Ferdinand was particularly occupied with Columbus and his expedition, the king ordered his treasurer-general Gabriel Sanchez to pay 30,000 florins in gold to "his beloved councillor and

---

* " Vos fueron recibidos é pagados en cuenta un cuento é ciento é cuarenta mil maravedis que distes por nuestro mandado al Obispo de Avila, que agora es Arzobispo de Granada, para el despacho del Almirante D. Cristóbal Colón."

" Dió y pagó mas el dicho Alonso de las Cabezas (Tesorero de la Cruzada en el obispado de Badajoz) por otro libramiento del dicho Arzobispo de Granada, fecho 5 de mayo de 92 años á Luis de Santangel, escribano de racion del Rey nuestro Señor, e por el á Alonso de Angulo, por virtud de un poder que del dicho escribano de racion mostró, en el cual estaba inserto dicho libramiento, docientos mil maravedis, en cuenta de cuatrocientos mil que en el, en Vasco de Quiroga, le libró el dicho Arzobispo por el dicho libramiento de dos cuentos seiscientos cuarenta mil maravedis, que hobo de haber en esta manera : un cuento é quinientos mil maravedis para pagar á Don Isag Abrahan por otro tanto que prestó á sus Altezas para los gastos de la guerra, é el un cuento ciento cuarenta mil maravedis restantes para pagar al dicho escribano de racion en cuenta de otro tanto que prestó para la paga de las carabelas que sus Altezas mandaron ir de Armada á las Indias, é para pagar á Cristóbal Colón que va en la dicha armada." *Contradurias generales*, epoc. I, num. 118, in Navarrete, *Coleccion de los Viages*, ii. 5 ; *Coleccion de Documentos inéditos del Archivo de Indias*, xix. 456. The above-mentioned Don Isag Abrahan is D. Isaac Abravanel. The original manuscript has "Abraā," which Navarrete read "Abrahan."

escribano de racion Luis de Santangel." * This sum certainly included the remainder of the loan.

Recent Spanish writers contend that Santangel received 17,000 maravedis as interest, but this assertion is wholly untenable. Luis de Santangel and also his kinsman Gabriel Sanchez † were the most zealous patrons of Columbus. Both acted unselfishly and solely for the welfare of their country. By their energetic efforts they succeeded in having Columbus recalled to the royal palace. At length his long-cherished plan of a voyage of discovery became a realized fact.

---

* Document dated Barcelona, May 20, 1493. *Arch. de la Corona de Aragon*, Reg. 3616, fol. 169 dorse.

† Gabriel's relatives, like all who bore the name of Santangel, were persecuted by the Inquisition. His father, Pedro Sanchez, was burned in effigy in Saragossa in 1493 "por hereje apóstata judayçante;" and his brothers and sisters died at the stake as Jewish heretics.

CHAPTER VI.

EXPULSION OF THE JEWS FROM SPAIN—AGREEMENT OF SANTA FÉ—EXODUS OF THE JEWS—COLUMBUS'S PREPARATIONS AND DEPARTURE—PARTICIPATION OF THE JEWS IN THE EXPEDITION—GUANAHANI—LUIS DE TORRES—INDIANS AND ISRAELITES.

"AFTER the Spanish monarchs had expelled all the Jews from all their kingdoms and lands in January, in that same month they commissioned me to undertake the voyage to India with a properly equipped fleet." * These are the words with which Columbus begins his journal. Without a word of disapprobation he thus mentions the tragic event which affected the welfare of hundreds of thousands, and which must have produced a profound impression upon the naturally vivacious explorer. His apathetic words are indicative of his fanaticism. This trait he did not, however, import from Italy, which at that time was a preëminently republican and commercial

---

* "Así que despues de haber echado fuera todos los Judíos de todos vuestros reinos y señoríos, en el mismo mes de Enero mandaron vuestras Altezas á mí que con armada suficiente me fuese á las dichas partidas de India." Navarrete, *Coleccion de los Viages*, i. 2; Las Casas, *Historia de las Indias*, cap. 26, i. 262.

country. A very different spirit was displayed by his countryman Agostino Giustiniani, the learned Bishop of Nebbio, who speaks of the Jews expelled from Spain with heartfelt sympathy.* He was the first to write a short biographical sketch of the explorer; this sketch, which lauds Columbus, is given incidentally in the bishop's polyglot psalter, in the commentaries on the nineteenth Psalm. Columbus's religious enthusiasm soon degenerated into fanaticism in consequence of his contact with ecclesiastics—his truest and most useful friends—and in consequence of his intimate intercourse with men like the Bachelor Andrés Bernáldez † and Pedro Martyr d'Angleria, who boasts of the special friendship of Columbus. This fanaticism was also nourished by sordid avarice and the desire to promote his own material interests. In order to appear particularly pious, he even wore the dark-brown cowl of the Franciscans.

The expulsion of the Jews from Spain is closely connected with Columbus's expedition and with the discovery of America, not merely externally in point of time but also intrinsically. Not in January, as Columbus asserts in his journal, but

---

* *Annali della Repubblica di Genova illustrati con note dal Cav. G. B. Spotorno*, ii. 566.

† Bernáldez, the fanatical author of the *History of the Catholic Kings* was parson of the little town of Los Palacios. Columbus was his guest for a time.

on March 31, 1492, the Catholic monarchs sent forth from the palace of the Alhambra the edict that all Jews and Jewesses of every age should, on pain of death, leave all the kingdoms and lands of Spain within four months. The edict, which was signed by Ferdinand and Isabella, is of a wholly religious character, especially as regards the chief reason given for the act. The reason given is that, in spite of the incessant and most energetic efforts of the Inquisition, the Marranos were beguiled by those who adhered to Judaism to return to their old faith, and that this greatly imperilled the Catholic religion.* The Jews were generously allowed to take their property with them " by land and water," excepting gold, silver, coined money, and merchandise subject to the laws prohibiting exportation; they could thus take with them only such articles as could be freely exported.†

The king and queen acted in full accord, but Ferdinand played the chief rôle in the barbarous expulsion of the Jews. Hence the edict was not

---

* The edict of expulsion is printed in full by Amador de los Rios, *Historia de los Judíos*, iii. 603 sq.

† The following words are at the close of the edict :—" E assi mismos damos liçençia é facultad á los dichos judios é judias que puedan sacar fuera de todos los dichos nuestros reynos é señorios sus bienes é faciendas por mar é por tierra, en tanto que non seya oro, nin plata, nin moneda amonedada, nin las otras cosas vedadas por las leyes de nuestros reynos, salvo mercaderías que non seyan cosas vedadas ó encobiertas."

signed by the Castilian secretary of state, Gaspar Gricio, but by the secretary of state of Aragon, Juan de Coloma, an old confidant of the king. Recent Spanish historians readily admit that Ferdinand was led to adopt this measure more by economic and political reasons, more by the desire to promote his own material interests, than by the religious zeal which actuated Isabella.* The king needed plenty of money to carry out his plan of bringing new territory under his dominion. He took it from the Jews, who were wealthy, especially in Castile; some of them were worth as much as one or two million maravedis or more.† The Inquisition, which he had called into existence, and the expulsion of the Jews, which he had decreed, had one and the same object: the former aimed to secure the property of the secret Jews for the state treasury, the latter, under the cloak of religion, aimed to confiscate the property of those who openly professed to be Jews.

The Jews knew the avaricious Ferdinand and his secret plans. As in the case of the Marranos

---

* "La expulsión de los Judíos obedeció menos á causas religiosas que á económicas y políticas," says Abdón de Paz in *Revista de España*, vol. 109, p. 377. See also Adolfo de Castro, *Historia de los Judíos en España*, 136, and Bofarull y Broca, *Historia crítica de Cataluña* [Barcelona, 1877], pp. 377 sq.

† Andrés Bernáldez, *Historia de los Reyes Católicos* [Seville, 1870], i. 341.

when the Inquisition was introduced, so now those over whose heads the Damoclesian sword of expulsion was hanging, made an attempt to purchase the king's consent to the withdrawal of the edict. Don Isaac Abravanel—whose self-sacrificing services on behalf of the state were acknowledged and to whom the king and queen still owed a large sum of money, borrowed during the war with the Moors*—offered Ferdinand 30,000 ducats if he would avert the evil that threatened the Jews. Whether Luis de Santangel—then in friendly intercourse with Abravanel—or Juan Cabrero, or other Marranos interceded with the king, is very doubtful. They were, on the one hand, more or less concerned in the matter, and feared to lose their lives if they interfered; on the other hand, they knew the king's obstinacy and avarice only too well. In fact, nothing could induce him to be merciful enough to recall the edict. On April 30, 1492, trumpets were sounded and the alcaldes publicly announced in Santa Fé and everywhere throughout the kingdom at one and the same time that by the end of July all Jews and Jewesses with their possessions should leave Spain, on pain of death and confiscation of their property by the

---

* See above, pages 77, 73.

state.* After that date no Spaniard was to harbor a Jew in his house or render him any assistance.

On April 30th, the very day on which the expulsion of the Jews was everywhere publicly announced,† Columbus was ordered to equip a fleet for his voyage to the Indies, and at the same time he received the contract which on April 17th had been arranged in Santa Fé between him and Juan de Coloma, the latter acting on behalf of the Spanish sovereigns.‡ Ferdinand, who had long energetically opposed the expedition, was

---

* "En último de Abril se pregonó con tres trompetas, Rey de Armas, dos Alcaldes, dos Alguaciles en el real de S. Fé sobre Granada . . . así mesmo de los reinos del Rey é de la Reyna, nuestros Señores, desde este dia fasta en fin del mes de Julio próximo inclusive, todos los Judios y Judias con sus personas é bienes sopena de muerte y de confiscacion para el fisco é cámara de sus Altezas. E este mesmo dia se habia de pregonar en todos los reinos y señoríos de los dichos Reyes, nuestros Señores." *Cronicon de Valladolid,* in *Documentos inéditos para la historia de España,* xiii. 192. Zacuto is in complete accord with this statement. In his *Jochasin,* p. 277, he says: "At the end of April trumpets were sounded in all the provinces and it was publicly announced that all Jews were to leave the kingdom within three months."

† Columbus's erroneous statement (see above, page 81) appears to be due to a slip of the pen; instead of "January" we must read "April." He confused the proclamation made at the end of April with the expulsion itself.

‡ This agreement is printed by Las Casas, *Historia de las Indias,* cap. 33; *Documentos inéditos . . . de América,* xxix. 422 sq.

obliged to yield, thanks to Columbus's persistency, and was obliged to accept the explorer's excessive demands, which had twice caused the negotiations to be discontinued. He granted him the title of admiral, with all its privileges, and made him viceroy and governor-general of all lands which he might discover or acquire. Columbus was not content with dignities and honors for himself and his descendants. He desired also to derive considerable material profit from his voyages. The chief aim of his explorations was, in fact, to find gold, and in a letter to the queen he frankly declared that this gold might even be the means of purifying the souls of men and of securing their entrance into Paradise. Thus he stipulated that he was to have a tenth of all pearls, precious stones, gold, silver, spices, and other wares,—in short, a tenth of everything found, bought, bartered, or otherwise obtained in the newly discovered lands; he was also to have an additional eighth of the profits of the present enterprise and of all similar ventures undertaken in the future, provided he should contribute an eighth of the expense.

Columbus now made preparations for his voyage. He went from Granada directly to the little port of Palos, which for some delinquency had been ordered by Ferdinand and his consort to equip two caravels within ten days. There he soon enlisted in behalf of his enterprise the services of the rich brothers Pinzon, who enjoyed a very high reputation among navigators. In Palos he also secured his sailors and travelling companions.

The Jews, under the ban of expulsion, made preparations to leave the beautiful land which for centuries had been the cherished home of their ancestors, and to which they were passionately attached. They arranged their public and private affairs, tried to sell their real and personal property, and to secure the payment of their outstanding debts; but only in a very few cases did they succeed in disposing of their property or in obtaining money from their debtors. As the day of departure approached, their sorrows increased. They spent whole nights on the graves of their ancestors, and they were particularly anxious that the cemeteries, which held the dearest of all their abandoned possessions, should be protected from desecration.

On August 2, 1492, which fell on the day of mourning for the two-fold destruction of Jerusalem, 300,000 Jews (according to some writers the number was much larger)* left Spain to settle in

---

* A rabbi, whose sagacity is extolled, "que llamaban Zentolla y al cual yo pusó nombre Tristan Bogado," informed Bernáldez that there were more than 1,160.000 Jews in Spain at the time of their expulsion. Andrés Bernáldez, *Historia de los Reyes Católicos*, i. 338.

Africa, Turkey, Portugal, Italy, and France. On that ever memorable day they sailed from the harbors of Cartagena, Valencia, Cadiz, Laredo, Barcelona, and Tarragona.*

---

* "En 2 de Agosto llegaron á la presente playa de Barcelona nueve fustas de gavia, entre ellas una nave del Tesoro y galera de Francia, y otros balleneros, y caravelas, en las que había reunidas mas de cuatro mil almas de judíos los cuales se habian embarcado en Tarragona." Bofarull y Broca, *Historia de Cataluña*, 376.

"Look, they move ! No comrades near but curses ;
Tears gleam in beards of men sore with reverses ;
Flowers from fields abandoned, loving nurses,
    Fondly deck the women's raven hair.

Faded, scentless flowers that shall remind them
Of their precious homes and graves behind them ;
Old men, clasping Torah-scrolls, unbind them,
    Lift the parchment flags, and silent lead.

'Mock not with thy light, O sun, our morrow,
Cease not, cease not, O ye songs of sorrow !
From what land a refuge can we borrow,
    Weary, thrust-out, God-forsaken we ?

'Where, oh ! where is rest for thy long-hated,
Hunted folk, whose fate in death unsated ?
Oh ! where is God ?' So swelled the wail unbated,
    From the mountains down unto the sea.

Could ye, suff'ring souls, peer through the Future,
From despair ye would awake to rapture :
Lo ! The Genoese boldly steers to capture
    Freedom's realm beyond an unsailed sea ! "

Thus wrote the German poet Ludwig August Frankl in his *Christ. Colombo* [Stuttgart, 1836]. He was the first Jew who sang

On August 2d the Spanish Jews began their wanderings, and the next day, Friday, August 3d, Columbus with his fleet of three ships, the *Santa María*, *Pinta*, and *Niña*, sailed to seek an ocean-route to India, and to discover a new world. He was accompanied on his first voyage by not more than one hundred and twenty men (according to some writers, by only ninety), almost all Castilians and Aragonese; many of them were from Palos, and some from Guadalajara, Avila, Segovia, Caceres, Castrojeriz, Ledesma, Villar, and Talavera— all cities in which before the expulsion large or small Jewish communities existed.

Were there any persons of Jewish extraction on the armada which under Columbus's guidance steered its course toward a new world? It was not easy for him to find men willing to accompany him on his adventurous voyage; even persons guilty of crime were released from prison on condition that they should enroll themselves among the recruits. What was to prevent Jews

---

of Columbus's heroic voyage. His epic is dedicated to King Carlo Alberto as Duke of Genoa. [The translator of this volume acknowledges his obligations to Mrs. Minnie D. Louis for the English version of the extract given above.]

Another Jew, Baron Albert Franchetti, nephew of Albert de Rothschild of Vienna, has composed an opera entitled *Cristoforo Colombo, Opera in tre atti;* the libretto was written by V. Penço, a Jew of Spanish origin [Genoa, 1883].

under the ban of expulsion, persecuted and homeless, from taking part in the voyage? Among the explorer's companions whose names have come down to us—the complete list is lost—there were several men of Jewish stock; for example, Luis de Torres, a Jew who had occupied a position under the governor of Murcia and who was baptized shortly before Columbus sailed. As he understood Hebrew, Chaldee, and some Arabic, Columbus employed him as interpreter.* Alonso de la Calle was also of Jewish lineage; his name was derived from the Jew's Lane, from which he came; he died in Española, May 23, 1503.† Rodrigo Sanchez of Segovia was a relative of the treasurer Gabriel Sanchez, and he took part in the first voyage at the particular request of Queen Isabella. The ship-physician Maestre Bernal and the surgeon (*surjano*) Marco were also of Jewish stock. Bernal had formerly lived in Tortosa, and as an adherent of Judaism, *por la Ley de Moysen*, had undergone public penance at Valencia in October, 1490, at the same time as Solomon Adret and his wife Isabel were burned.‡

When the fleet, whose crew was a very mixed

---

* Herrera, *Historia General*, dec. 1, lib. 23.

† Navarrete, *Coleccion de los Viages*, i. 294.

‡ Inquisition records of Valencia, now in the archives of Alcalá de Henares.

body of men—Spaniards, Moors, and Jews, as well as an Irishman and a Genoese—had covered more than two thousand miles, the seamen began to murmur loudly at the intolerable length of the voyage. Columbus calmed them as well as he could. On October 11th after the customary evening hymn, he admonished his crew to keep a sharp look-out for land. In addition to the gratuity of ten thousand maravedis offered by the king, he promised a silk waistcoat to him who should first sight land. At last, early on Friday morning, October 12th—the day on which the Jews expelled from Spain and their co-religionists in every part of the world were singing their hosannas*—the cry "*Tierra, Tierra*" ("Land, Land") arose from the *Pinta*.

In his journal Columbus confesses that land was first seen by one of his sailors; but the avaricious explorer could not withstand the temptation to claim the royal gratuity of ten thousand maravedis, and the poor sailor lost this as well as the promised waistcoat. Who was the fortunate mariner whose hopes were thus shattered? Gonçalo Fernandez de Oviedo, who saw the Jews depart from Spain and heard their doleful lamentations, was informed (so he tells us) by Vicente Pinzon, the commander of the *Niña*, and by the

---

* It was "hosanna rabbah," a day on which the Jews recited many prayers beginning with the word "hosanna."

seaman Hernan Perez Matheos, that it was a sailor from Lepe who first saw a distant light and cried " Land." According to Oviedo, when this man found that he had been defrauded of the gratuity, he obtained his discharge, went to Africa, and there discarded Christianity for his old faith. The chronicler does not inform us whether the old faith was Judaism.* According to others, it was Rodrigo de Triana, a sailor of the *Pinta*, who first cried " Land."

The land was Watling's Island or perhaps Acklin Island; the natives called it Guanahani. We are told that it was given this name by the Spanish Jews on board the *Pinta*, and Guanahani is even said to be formed from Hebrew words. A professor of the Oriental languages in Tacubaya, who comes from Mahón on the island of Minorca and who calls Isaac Abravanel his ancestor, claims to have been led to this etymological discovery by a Spanish ballad, which, he asserts, he received from Spanish Jews in Barbary. According to this ballad, in which there is a sprinkling of Hebrew and Arabic words, as soon as Rodrigo de Triana saw

---

* " . . . porque no se le dieron las albricias . . . se passo en Affricay y renego la fé;" Oviedo, *Coron. de las Indias* [1547], cap. 5, pag. 7. " I asi el marinero de Lepe se pasó en Berberia y ali renego la fé;" Gómara, *Historia de las Indias.* 163; Oviedo, *Historia general y natural de las Indias* [Madrid, 1851], i. 24.

land he uttered the little Hebrew word "*I, I*" ("Island, Island"), to one of his Jewish comrades. The latter then asked in the same language "*W'an-nah?*" ("And where?"). Thereupon Triana responded "*Hen-i*" ("There is the island"). Thus originated the name "Uanaheni" or "Guanahani."* This childish explanation of the word is not worthy of serious consideration. Rodrigo de Triana was not a Jew, nor did he speak Hebrew, and Guanahani is known to be a word of Indian origin.

Columbus took possession of this island for the ruler of Castile, and then, sailing southwest to Fernandina, discovered the island which he named Isabella in honor of the queen. Still searching for the island of Cipango with its fabulous wealth of gold and spices, he reached Cuba by the end of October. He believed that he was in the immediate neighborhood of the Great Khan's kingdom, and he determined to send envoys into the interior to ascertain, as he expressed it in a letter to Luis de Santangel, whether a king or great cities were there. This mission he entrusted to Luis de Torres, who was accompanied by Rodrigo de Jerez of Ayamonte.† Columbus gave them specific instruc-

---

* F. Rivas Puigcerver, *Los Judíos y el Nuevo Mundo* [Mexico, 1891]. See also *Boletín de la real Academia de la Historia*, xix. 364, and xx. 215 sq.

† Harrisse, *Chr. Colomb*, i. 421, 437.

tions, ordered them to prepare the way for a treaty of peace between the ruler of the country and the Castilian crown, and gave them a letter and presents for the former. They also took with them samples of pepper and other spices, in order to show them to the natives and ascertain where such things grew. On Friday, November 2d, Luis de Torres and his companion began their journey into the unknown land, and returned to Columbus on the sixth. They reported that, after travelling sixty miles, they came to a place with fifty huts and with a population of about one thousand persons; here they found men and women with fire in their hands, with which they lit one end of a small roll held in the mouth; it resembled dried leaves and was called *tabaco;* * they inhaled the other end of the little roll, and blew forth great clouds of smoke through the mouth and nose. The two envoys received a very friendly welcome from the natives and their chief; the women kissed their hands and feet, and when they departed they were escorted by the ruler, his son, and more than five hundred persons.†

---

* "Hallaron . . . por el camino mucha gente que atravesaba á sus pueblos, mugeres y hombres, con un tizon en la mano, yerbas para tomar sus sahumerios que acostumbraban." Navarrete, *Coleccion de los Viages*, i. 51.

† Franc. Ad. de Varnhagen, *La verdadera Guanahani de Colon* [Santiago, 1864], pp. 31 sq.

Luis de Torres, the first European who discovered the use of tobacco, was also the first person of Jewish stock who settled in Cuba. He won the favor of the ruler, the cacique, and received from him as presents not merely lands but also slaves—five adults and a child.* The king and queen of Spain granted him a yearly allowance of 8,645 maravedis,† and he died in the newly discovered land.‡

In Cuba, Española, and the other islands which he discovered, Columbus found natives who had their caciques, and their own language and traditions. To what race did these aborigines of America belong? Several writers have asserted, and have displayed much learning in attempting to prove, that the aborigines were descendants of the Jews.§ This result was reached already in the sixteenth century by the Spanish clergyman Roldan; his arguments were derived from an unpublished manuscript which he discovered in

---

* "Luis de Torres . . . en el dicho cacique un niño . . . cinco viejos que no son de servicio." *Documentos inéditos del Archivo de Indias*, i. 87.

† *Arch. de Indias*, 39, 2, ½. The allowance of Maestre Alonso *físico* was 11,188 maravedis.

‡ Ces. Fernández Duro, *Estudios auxiliares para reconstitución de la nao Santa María* [Madrid, 1892], p. 61.

§ Among other writers, see Gaffarel, *Histoire de la découverte de l'Amérique* [Paris, 1892], i. 89 sq.

the Library of S. Pablo in Seville.* Montesinos,†
who possessed the manuscripts of Luis Lopez, the
learned Bishop of Quito, was convinced that the
Peruvians were of Jewish origin. The view of
Roldan and of Gregorio Garcia,‡ that the aborigines of America were descendants of the Jews,
was maintained with many arguments in one and
the same year, 1650, independently by the Englishman Thorowgood § and by the Portuguese Jew
Manasseh ben Israel, a renowned rabbi of Amsterdam who induced Cromwell to allow the Jews
to return to England. A Portuguese Marrano of
Villaflor, who, strange to say, also called himself
Montesinos and afterwards assumed the name
Aaron Levi, informed Manasseh that he had
mingled in South America with Jews of the Ten
Tribes. Manasseh's book attracted much attention and was translated into Latin, Spanish,
Dutch, English, Italian, and Hebrew.‖ Nor has
interest in it ceased even at the present day;

---

* See Appendix viii.

† He was a fiery and fearless clergyman, who for a long time resided in Lima early in the sixteenth century.

‡ Greg. Garcia, *Origen de los Indios de el Nuevo Mondo* [Valencia, 1607].

§ Thorowgood, *Jews in America; or Probabilities that the Americans are of that Race* [London, 1650].

‖ Menasse ben Israel, *Esperança de Israel* [Amsterdam, 1650; 2d edition, Smyrna, 1659]. The Latin translation is entitled *Spes Israelis* [anno 1650].

this treatise "on the origin of the Americans" was reprinted twelve years ago by the Spaniard Santágo Perez Junquera.* The descent of the Americans is, in fact, a question which has often been discussed since the discovery of America down to the present day. Even in recent times the Englishman Lord Kingsborough devoted his time, his attainments, and the greater part of his large fortune to the publication of a collection of American documents, in order to prove the Jewish origin of the Americans.†

It is not improbable that the Jews who were driven from Nineveh by Salmanassar wandered into uninhabited regions. According to Herrera, the Indians cherished the tradition that Yucatan had been settled by tribes from the Orient. Several writers give the exact route by which the Jews travelled until they settled in Cuba. Lord Kingsborough even asserts that they crossed Behring Straits, and then proceeded to Mexico and Peru.

---

* Junquera, *Esperanza de Israel. Reimpresión del libro . . . sobre el orígen de los Americanos* [Madrid, 1881]. Rabbi Louis Grossmann of Detroit, Mich., translated a part of the work into English, in the *American Jews' Annual* for the year 5649, i.e. 1889, under the title *The Origin of the American Indians and the Lost Ten Tribes* [New York, Chicago, and Cincinnati: Leo Wise & Co.].

† *Antiquities of Mexico* [London, 1830–1848], vol. vi.

Of more interest than the mode of migration is the question whether any analogies in language, in traditions, in religious conceptions, or in religious ceremonies justify the acceptance of this ethnological theory. Roldan's chief argument in support of his view is the language of the Indians in Española, Cuba, Jamaica, and the adjoining islands. He contends that it has many resemblances to Hebrew; in fact, he even calls it corrupted Hebrew. He asserts that such names as Cuba and Hayti are Hebrew, and that they were first applied by the earliest caciques, the chiefs or leaders (*Kasin*), who discovered and peopled the islands. The names of rivers and of persons in use among the natives are derived from the Hebrew: for example, Haina from the Hebrew Ain, stream, Yones from Jona, Yaque from Jacob, Ures from Urias, Siabao from Siba, Maisi from Moysi. The names of their tools, of their little canoes or *cansas*, the name *axi* for pepper, the name of the store-house for maize, grain, and the like, all point to the Hebrew language.*

Their rites and ceremonies, as well as their language, form one of the main arguments in favor of this theory of descent. Circumcision prevailed among the Indians; they often bathed in rivers

---

* See Appendix viii.

and streams; they refrained from touching the dead and from tasting blood; they had definite fast-days; marriage with sisters-in-law was permitted if they were childless widows; wives were discarded for new helpmates. They also sacrificed first fruits on high mountains and under shady trees; they had temples and carried a holy ark before them in time of war; they were also, like the Ten Tribes, inclined to idol worship.* All writers and travellers agree, moreover, that there were many Jewish types of face among the Indians, the aborigines of America.

The question whether the American Indians are descendants of the Jews, whether they are the offspring of "the lost Ten Tribes," has often been answered in both the affirmative and the negative,† but it has not yet been definitely settled.

---

* See Appendix viii.

† See, among other writers, Garrick Mallery, *Israelite and Indian; a Parallel in Planes of Culture* [Salem, 1889]; translated into German by F. S. Krauss [Leipzig, 1892]. For other works on this subject, see *Narrative and Critical History of America*, edited by Justin Winsor [Boston, 1889], i. 115, 116.

CHAPTER VII.

Columbus's Return—His Letters to Santangel and Sanchez—Preparations for the Second Expedition; the Money of the Jews Utilized—The Second Voyage—Portuguese Discoveries—Vasco da Gama and Abraham Zacuto—Gaspar da Gama—Francisco d'Albuquerque and Hucefe, or Alexander d'Atayde.

DELIGHTED with the success of his expedition and with the great treasures of gold, silver, and spices which he had found, Columbus began his return voyage in January, 1493. He gratefully remembered that Luis de Santangel had furnished him with the means of undertaking his journey, and hence he regarded it as his duty to send Santangel the first glad tidings of his success—a detailed account of his voyage and discoveries. This letter was written in Spanish near the Azores or the Canaries on February 15, 1493. In it Columbus spoke of the great triumph which God had vouchsafed to him, and stated that he and the armada which the Spanish monarch had placed at his disposal had reached the Indies in twenty-three days, and that he had there discovered many inhabited islands.* He made a

---

* His letter to Luis de Santangel is printed by Navarrete, *Coleccion de los Viages*, i. 167–174.

similar report to the treasurer Gabriel Sanchez. Santangel and Sanchez immediately forwarded these letters to the king and queen, who were then residing at Barcelona, and soon afterwards their majesties received the explorer with much ceremony.

The news of the discoveries rapidly spread through the greater part of Europe.* Gabriel

---

* Columbus and the Spanish discoveries early attracted the attention of Jewish writers. The first of them who mentions the subject is Abraham Farisol of Avignon, who, when nineteen years of age, settled in Mantua, and thence migrated to Ferrara. Here he was appointed cantor of the Jewish community, and he also devoted himself to active literary work. In his leisure moments he studied natural science and cosmography. The accounts of Columbus's discoveries which were first published at Vicenza, in 1507, in a collection of travels in the New World, served as the basis of Farisol's work entitled *Letter on the Ways of Life*. It was written in Hebrew in November, 1524, and was first published in Venice in 1587. It was reprinted with a Latin translation by Thomas Hyde in 1691. This work, which is a sort of general treatise on geography, gives some brief notices concerning America, and calls the discoverer " Cristofol Colombo, a Genoese."

This subject was studied more thoroughly by Joseph Cohen, a son of Spanish exiles, who was born in Avignon in 1495. He was educated in Genoa, where he practised as a physician until 1550, when he and his coreligionists were banished from that city. He went to Voltaggio, where he remained eighteen years, and then settled in Costelleto in Montferrat. He was eighty years old when he died. He translated into Hebrew the *Historia general de las Indias*, by Francisco Lopez de Gómara, which appeared in 1535, and the second part of which contains *La Conquista de Mexico y de la Nueva España*. The Hebrew translation is in two books : " The Book of India," and " The Book of Fernando Cor-

Sanchez gave a copy of Columbus's letter to a bookseller in Barcelona, who had it printed in Gothic characters; within a year two editions were published. Leandro de Cosco prepared a Latin translation, of which four editions were printed in the first year, 1493. In recent years several English and Italian translations of these letters have been published.* They will always

---

tes," or "The Book of Mexico." The translation, which was completed in 1557, exists only in manuscript. See *Revue des Études Juives*, xvi. 30 sq. Cohen also deals with the Portuguese and Spanish discoveries in his Hebrew treatise entitled, *Book of the Chronicle of the Kings of France and of the Ottoman Grand-Dukes*, which first appeared in Venice in 1553 or 1554. It was reprinted in Amsterdam in 1733, and was translated into English by Bialloblotzky, under the title, *The Chronicles of R. Joseph ben Joshua the Sephardi* [London, 1834-36]. The passages relating to the Spanish explorations were reprinted by Dr. A. Kohut in *The Menorah*, xiii. 417 sq. Cohen ascribes the discovery of America to Amerigo Vespucci.

* For Italian translations of both letters, see *Raccolta completa dellig scritti di Crist. Colombo . . . di Giov. Batt. Torre* [1864], pp. 214-229; and *Lettera in lingua spagnuola dir. da Crist. Colombo á Luis de Santangel, riprod. ed illustr. p. Gerol. D'Adda* [Milan, 1866]. Both letters are printed in *Notes on Columbus* by H. Harrisse [New York, 1866], pp. 89 sq., 101 sq. See also *Letters of Columbus to Luis de Santangel*, 1493 [New York, 1864]; *Columbus's Spanish Letter to Luis de Santangel, escribano de racion of the kingdom of Aragon, reprinted in facsimile, translated and edited from the unique copy of the original* [London, 1891]; *The first Letter of Chr. Columbus to the noble lord Raphael Sanchez, reproduced in facsimile from the copy of the Latin version of 1493 now in the Boston Public Library* [Boston, 1891. Edited by Henry W. Haynes].

form the most remarkable memorial of American history.

In order to guard against the jealousy of Portugal, and to secure for Spain the lands discovered by Columbus as well as those that he might discover in the future, the wily Ferdinand appealed to the pope for assistance. At that time the papal throne was occupied by the Aragonese Alexander VI. The only good thing that can be said of him is that he treated the Jews magnanimously; he was, in fact, commonly called "the Marrano," or "the Jew."* Though he was not a friend of Ferdinand, he issued his celebrated Bull of Demarcation on May 3, 1493, which aimed to prevent future quarrels between Spain and Portugal regarding the possession of newly discovered territory. This concession was granted to Spain for all future time, on condition that her rulers should strive to propagate the Catholic faith in the newly discovered lands.†

While Columbus was yet in Barcelona, rapid preparations were made for his second voyage. Ferdinand did not now lack means. According to his own statement, he had ascertained that

---

* Döllinger, *Beiträge zur Geschichte des* 16. *Jahrhunderts*, iii. 383; Valent. Nemec, *Papst Alexander VI.* [Klagenfurt, 1879.]

† This concession was subsequently modified by the Treaty of Tordesillas.

the Jews, expelled from his kingdom " for the honor and glory of God," had left behind them money or its equivalent in real and personal property, as well as many debts which they had been unable to collect. According to a royal order of November 23, 1492, the authorities were to confiscate for the state treasury all property which had belonged to the Jews, including that which Christians had taken from them, or had appropriated unlawfully or by violence.* On May 23, 1493, the admiral of the newly discovered islands and Juan Rodriguez de Fonseca, Archdeacon of Seville, who was supervising the equipment of the fleet on behalf of the crown, were ordered to go to Seville and Cadiz for the purpose of securing such ships, seamen, and provisions as were needed for the second expedition.† On the same day Ferdinand and Isabella signed a large number of injunctions to royal officers in Soria, Zamora, Burgos, and many other cities,

---

* The document, dated Saragossa, November 23, 1492, begins as follows : " Ferdinandus Rex delectis meis Jacobo Casafranca et Benedicto Ginneu salutem et delectionem. Tempore expulsionis Judeorum nostri edicti et imperii ad honorem et gloriam Majestatis domini facto ab omnibus Regnis et terris nostris intelleximus ab ipsis Judeis sub ipso recessu varias et diversas pecunias esse extortas," etc. *Arch. de la Corona de Aragon*, Reg. 3552, fol. 162.

† The document is dated Barcelona, May 23, 1493; see Appendix ix.

directing them to secure immediate possession of all the money, precious metals, gold and silver utensils, jewels, gems, and everything else that had been taken from Jews who had been expelled from Spain or who had migrated to Portugal, and everything that these Jews had entrusted for safe-keeping to Marrano relatives or friends, and all Jewish possessions which Christians had found or had unlawfully appropriated. The royal officers were also ordered to convert all this property into ready money and to give the proceeds to the treasurer Francisco Pinelo in Seville, to meet the expenses of Columbus's second expedition.*

The large sums of money which had been taken from the banished Jews were thus appropriated by the crown. For example, several bills of exchange which Juan Bran, a Jew who had fled to Portugal, was to pay for Antonio de Castro of Toledo to Julian Catanes and Bernaldo Pinolo, were found in the possession of various merchants, and were confiscated by the crown. The proceeds, 4,120 ducats in gold, were deposited in the monastery of Las Cuevas by De la Torre, an officer of the royal treasury. On May 23, 1493, the king and queen requested the Count of Cifuentes to take the money from the monastery at once and have it safely transferred to the treas-

---
* See Appendix x.–xvii.

urer Pinelo, in order that he might use it for the equipment of the fleet which was to be sent to the Indies.* Juan de Ocampo, the Alcaide of Orueña, had in his possession gold, ornaments, clothing, and other articles, abandoned by a Jew who had fled to Portugal. A detailed inventory of this property, drawn up by the royal secretary Fernando Alvares de Toledo and signed by other royal officers, was sent to Count Alonso, a kinsman of Ferdinand and Isabella; he was instructed to take charge of the articles, to sell them, and to give the proceeds, by the end of June or at the latest by July 10th, to Pinelo, to help pay the expenses of the armada which was to be equipped "for the discovery of the islands and continents in the ocean."† In like manner and for the same purpose Bernaldino de Lerma was ordered to transfer to Pinelo the cash equivalent of the money, valuables, clothing, and other articles belonging to the banished Jews which the king's bailiff Juan de Soria, the wife of Diego Guiral, Antonio Gomez de Sevilla, Alvaro de Ledesma, and others had received from the goldsmith Diego de Medina of Zamora. Bernaldino received an order to deal in like manner with all the gold, silver, jewels, and

---

* Appendix x.

† For the decrees, dated May 20 and May 23, 1493, and the inventory, see Appendix xi. and xii.

various other things (specified in an inventory sent with the order) which Rabbi Ephraim,* the richest Jew in Burgos, had, before migrating from Spain, left with Isabel Osorio, the wife of Luis Nuñez Coronel of Zamora.†

Not merely the clothing, ornaments, and valuables which had been taken from the fugitive Jews were converted into money, but also the debts which they had been unable to recover were declared by order of the crown to be forfeited to the state treasury, and stringent measures were adopted to collect them. Several merchants in Calahorra, Burgos, and other cities, namely, Alonso de Lerma, Juan de Torres, Alonso de Salamanca, Juan Alonso de Sahagund, and others, owed large sums of money to the wealthy Ephraim and to Benveniste of Calahorra, who at the time of the expulsion was an inhabitant of Burgos. Garcia de Herrera, an officer of the royal household, was ordered to collect these debts at once, as well as all other debts which the Jews had left behind them within the territory of Burgos, or at least such of these claims as had not already been paid to the *corregidor* Garcia Cortés. In like manner Luis Nuñez

---

* In contemporary documents he is sometimes called Rabi Frayn, or Rubifrayn.

† See Appendix xv.–xvii.

Coronel was commanded to pay to Bernaldino de Lerma, without further opposition or delay, the 4,850 ducats which his wife owed for houses bought from the Jews.*

The above-mentioned inventories of the confiscated articles found in the hands of Christians or in the hands of Marrano kinsmen of the banished Jews† enable us to estimate approximately the wealth of the Jews, as well as the avarice of the Spanish rulers. Among the possessions of the Jews we find spoons, cups, bowls, kettles, pots, candlesticks, canes, all of silver, also silver and gold rings, pearls and corals, a surprisingly large number of silver bracelets, brooches, belts, chains, buckles, buttons, and head-bands. ‡ In their boundless avarice the king and queen ordered not

---

* See Appendix xvi. For the order sent to Garcia de Herrera, dated Barcelona, May 24, 1493, see *Coleccion de Documentos inéditos rel. al descubrimiento de las antiguas posesiones de América*, xxx. 77–91 : "Para Garcia Cortés corregidor de Burgos en rrempuesta de lo que escrebió . . . de las debdas que le ocurrian cerca de la cobranza de las debdas que dexaron los judios en la dicha cibdad e su tierra y en otras partes que quedó a cargo de cobrar a vecinos de la dicha cibdad."

† From the Marrano Iñigo de Ribas Altas, whose earlier name is not mentioned in the document, various silver articles were taken which belonged to his mother-in-law, a Jewess who remained in Portugal. See Appendix xv.

‡ The law forbade Jewish women to wear ornaments made of gold. See Kayserling, *Das Castilianische Gemeinde-Statut*, in *Jahrbuch für die Geschichte der Juden*, iv. 278, 331.

merely all the confiscated valuables and clothing of the Jews to be sold, but also the threadbare damask, velvet, silk, and linen coverings and mantles of the *Torah* rolls, and the silk table-covers used in the synagogues; they were all utilized for the equipment of Columbus's expedition.

It is quite certain that the measures adopted by Ferdinand and Isabella for Soria, Zamora, and Burgos were also applied to all other cities and provinces in which Jews had lived. From the inventories which are still extant we may infer that in cash alone—in the form of ducats, doubloons, reals, castellanos, florins, justos,* and cruzados—at least two million maravedis† were taken from the banished Jews. If we add to this the proceeds of the confiscated bills of exchange which came from Portugal, the large debts due the Jews in Burgos alone which the crown collected, and the proceeds of the many gold and silver articles, jewels and gems, specified as sequestered, the sum which the state treasury gained by the expulsion of the Jews—reckoned simply on the basis of the extant inventories—amounted to about six million maravedis. This was more than four times

---

* A justo is a Portuguese gold coin worth 600 reis; a half justo is called an espadin.

† In the time of Ferdinand and Isabella, 1 mark of silver = 2210 maravedis, 1 ducat = 383 maravedis, 1 doubloon = 490 maravedis.

as much as was expended on Columbus's first expedition.* To this sum must be added the two million which the Inquisition in Seville handed over to the Florentine merchant Juonato Beradi, who lived in Seville and who had been entrusted with the equipment of the armada.†

It is impossible to compute the enormous sums which the Inquisition wrested from the Jews and Moors, or which the state treasury gained by the expulsion of the Jews. Poor Spain! According to an order of May 23, 1493, it was from the money of the Jews that Columbus was paid the ten thousand maravedis which the Spanish monarchs had promised as a reward to him who should first sight land; and on May 24th he received an additional gift of a thousand doubloons from the same source.‡ As we have already pointed out, it was also with Jewish gold that the expenses of his second expedition were paid.

On May 28, 1493, Columbus left Barcelona to make the necessary preparations for his second

---

* Cf. Harrisse, *Ch. Colomb*, i. 396.

† "Las Caraveles, que os escrivimos, havian de ir á Indias dara Juonato Beradi por los precios que vereis: el obispo de Avila escriuio á los Inquisidores de Sevilla que os diesen dos cuentos . . . y vaya muy presto que hay en Indias mucha necesidad." *Coleccion Muñoz* (*Biblioteca de la real Academia de la Historia en Madrid*), vol. 75, fol. 168.

‡ *Coleccion de Documentos . . . de América*, xxix. 492 sq.

great voyage, and he sailed from Cadiz for America on September 25th. He was accompanied by twelve hundred men, among whom there were, as in the case of the first voyage, several persons of Jewish lineage. The list of the crew has not come down to us.

Columbus discovered the islands of Dominica, Marigalante, Guadaloupe, and Porto Rico, and ultimately reached Jamaica; but he soon fell from the pinnacle of renown to which he had so laboriously climbed. The hidalgos who accompanied him were disappointed in their expectations; the success attained was not commensurate with the great cost of their voyage. The rulers of Spain, the distrustful Ferdinand and the fickle Isabella, withdrew from him their favor, until finally he fell into disgrace. This was partly due to the discoveries which the Portuguese made about that time.

Columbus's success had encouraged the Portuguese to continue their explorations along the south coast of Africa, in search of the land of precious stones and spices and an ocean-route to India. The plan which João II. had formed to undertake a new voyage of discovery, but which his death prevented him from executing, was taken up by his nephew and successor, Dom Manuel, soon after his accession to the throne. The commander whom he appointed to take charge of the squadron equipped for this purpose was Vasco da Gama, a man of great determination, well versed in cosmography and nautical science.

Before dispatching the flotilla, however, the king summoned his confidential astrologer to Beja, the royal residence, in order to consult with him once more concerning the plan of exploration. This astrologer was Abraham Zacuto, mentioned in a preceding chapter, who in consequence of the Spanish edict of expulsion of March 31, 1492, had followed his aged teacher, the pious rabbi Isaac Aboab, to Portugal, and had settled in Lisbon. Henceforth he devoted his services to the land which, at least for a while, hospitably received him and his Spanish co-religionists. On account of his extensive knowledge of astronomy and mathematics, he was highly esteemed by both King João and Dom Manuel. In 1494 João made him an honorary present of ten espadins in gold, or three thousand reis;* Manuel appointed him his astrologer, and had frequent conferences with him concerning astronomical and maritime matters. At King Manuel's request, Zacuto devoted himself with much zeal to the elaboration of a

---

* Ribeiro dos Santos, *Sobre algunos mathematicos Portuguezes*, in *Memorias da literatura Portugueza*, viii. 163.

theory concerning storms, and he indicated how ships could, without danger, make the voyage to the Cape of Good Hope and return in a comparatively short time.*

King Manuel showed his gratitude to Zacuto, and asked the latter's advice concerning the proposed expedition to India. The astrologer did not conceal from the king the great dangers which would have to be encountered in a journey to so distant a land, but he said that, in his opinion, it would result in the subjection of a large part of India to the Portuguese crown.† Zacuto's works materially facilitated the execution of the great plans of Vasco da Gama and other explorers. Da Gama held Zacuto in high esteem, and before sailing from Lisbon on July 8, 1497, conferred with him and received information from him in the presence of his whole crew.‡

During Da Gama's return voyage to Europe, while he was staying on the little island of Anchediva, sixty miles from Goa, a tall European with a long white beard approached his ship, in a boat with a small crew. He had been sent by his

---

* Gaspar Correa, *Lendas da India*, in *Collecção de monumentos ineditos para a historia dos Portuguezes*, i. 261 sq.

† *Ibid.*, i. 10.

‡ Before 1502 Zacuto went to Tunis, where he wrote his valuable chronicle, *Jochasin*. He died in Smyrna about the year 1515.

master Sabayo, the Moorish ruler of Goa, to negotiate with the foreign navigator. This visitor was a Jew, who, according to some chroniclers, came from Posen, according to others from Granada. Expelled from their homes on account of their religion, his parents had migrated to Turkey and Palestine. From Alexandria, which according to some chroniclers was his birthplace, he proceeded across the Red Sea to Mecca and thence to India. Here he was in captivity for a long time, and later was made admiral (*capitao mór*) by Sabayo. *

When the Jew reached the Portuguese vessels with their flying bunting, he greeted the fleet in the Castilian language with the nautical salutation, "God bless the ships, the captains, and all the sailors." Great was the joy of the Portuguese to hear so far from home a language closely related to their native speech. Great also was the desire of the Jew to obtain news from his native land, which still remained dear to him. Trusting to the promise of complete security which the

---

* According to Damião de Goes, *Chron. de D. Manuel*, pt. 1, cap. 44, "era judeu de Reyno do Polonia do Cidade de Posna." According to Barros, *Asia*, dec. 1, lib. 4, cap. 11, he was born in Alexandria. Correa, i. 125, calls him "judeo granadi . . . este judeo na tomada de Granada sendo homem mancebo desterrado;" this does not agree, however, with the Jew's own statement that before the arrival of the Portuguese in Goa, in 1498, he had spent forty years in prison. His name is unknown.

Portuguese gave him, he went on board one of their vessels. He was received with tokens of respect, and the sailors listened with pleasure to his reminiscences. His desire to prolong the conference led Vasco da Gama to suspect that he was a spy. On a signal from the commander, the Jew, much to his surprise, was suddenly seized, and bound hand and foot. After being disrobed, he was unmercifully flogged by two menials of the ship. Da Gama swore by the life of his king that he would have him flogged until he should confess the whole truth. To escape the torments of torture he finally went over to the Portuguese, and in order to save his life he promised to allow himself to be baptized. He was named Gaspar da Gama after the admiral, who acted as his godfather.

The Jewish mariner Gaspar, or as he is sometimes called Gaspar de las Indias, was taken to Lisbon by Vasco da Gama. King Manuel, who was much pleased with the newcomer and liked to converse with him, gave him rich presents of clothing, horses, and servants, and also granted him a charter of privileges.* As Peschel truly affirms,† Gaspar rendered inestimable services to Vasco da Gama and to several later commanders of the Portuguese fleet. He was a mariner of

---

* Correa, *Lendas da India,* i. 192.
† Peschel, *Geschichte des Zeitalters der Entdeckungen,* 575.

experience, well versed in languages and fully informed in all matters relating to India.*

In the year 1500 he accompanied Pedro Alvarez Cabral on his expedition to the East. This he did at the express desire of the king, who instructed Cabral to confer with Gaspar on all important matters. Cabral employed him chiefly as interpreter. Splendidly attired Gaspar negotiated with the King of Melinde, whose acquaintance he had already made when he was in the employ of Sabayo. By assuming the Moorish dress as a disguise and by pretending to pray like a Moslem, he discovered a rebellious plot of the natives of Calicut to massacre the Portuguese.†

From Calicut Cabral sailed southward to Cochin. Gaspar had advised him to do this. The Jew had expressed the opinion that, with favorable winds, Cochin could be reached in a single day. He had also informed the admiral that a better harbor and much more pepper and other spices would be found there than in Calicut.‡

At Cape Verd, on his homeward voyage, Cabral met the ships which had been sent from

---

* He also wrote an account of the scientific observations which he had made during his travels. *Paesi novam. retrovati* [Venice, 1507], cap. 61.

† Correa, *Lendas da India*, i. 163, 199.

‡ *Ibid.*, i. 209 sq. According to Correa, it was by following Gaspar's advice that Cabral discovered the coast of Brazil.

Portugal expressly to discover Brazil. Amerigo Vespucci, who was on this fleet, hastened to profit by the knowledge and experience of Gaspar da Gama, the best-informed man among Cabral's followers. Gaspar gave him the desired information concerning the situation and condition, the wealth and commerce, of the distant lands which Vespucci intended to visit. The latter, it may be incidentally observed, never mentions Columbus and his discoveries; he ignores him as if he had never existed. But he speaks of Gaspar in terms of high praise. In one of his letters Vespucci refers to him as "a trustworthy man who speaks many languages and knows the names of many cities and provinces, who made two voyages from Portugal to the Indian Ocean, and journeyed from Cairo to Malacca, a province on the coast of that ocean. He also visited the island of Sumatra, and he told me that he knew of a great kingdom in the interior of India which was rich in gold, pearls, and other precious stones."*

---

* ". . . . uno uomo degno di fede, che si chiamava Guaspare, che avea corso dal Cairo fino a una provincia che si domanda Malacca la quale sta situata alla costa del mare Indico . . . il detto Guaspare, el quale sapeva di molte lingue, e il nome di molte provincie e citta. Como dico é uomo molto altentico perche ha fatto due fiate el viaggio di Portogallo al mare Indico." F. A. de Varnhagen, *Amerigo Vespucci; son caractère, ses écrits, sa vie* [Lima, 1865]; Humboldt, *Examen critique de l'histoire de la géographie*, v. 82.

In the year 1502 Gaspar made another voyage to India with a fleet which was commanded by Vasco da Gama. He negotiated with the King of Quiloa, who was known to be cunning and artful. In Cochin, a few days later, he again found his wife. This woman, who was noted for her learning, had withstood all inducements to abandon Judaism.* When the first Viceroy of India, Francisco d'Almeida, went to take possession of his post in 1505, he was accompanied by Gaspar and, among others, by the son of Dr. Martin Pinheiro, the judge of the supreme court in Lisbon. Young Pinheiro carried with him a trunk entirely filled with *Torah* rolls, which had belonged to the recently destroyed synagogues of Portugal. He intended to sell them in Cochin, where there were many Jews and synagogues.† Gaspar's wife negotiated the sale; for thirteen *Torah* rolls Pinheiro obtained four thousand pardaos. When the viceroy heard of this transaction, he reproached Pinheiro in violent language, and then,

---

* "Gaspar . . . que em Cochym tinha huma judia, que fora sua molher, que elle nom pôde fazer que se tornasse Christã. Esta judia era grande letrada na ley." Correa, *Lendas da India*, i. 656.

† In 1504, when Isaac Abravanel wrote his commentaries on the Book of Jeremiah, he saw a letter, written by Portuguese merchants who came from India with spices. In this letter they stated that they had met many Jews in that land. Abravanel, *Commentaries on Jeremiah*, cap. 3.

after confiscating the proceeds of the sale for the state treasury, he immediately sent an account of the whole affair to Lisbon.*

Gaspar returned to Lisbon with Vasco da Gama in 1503. King Manuel, who still held him in high esteem, conferred upon him the rank of *cavalleiro de sua casa* in recognition of his services.

In a relation similar to that which Gaspar bore to Vasco da Gama, another Jew stood to Affonso d'Albuquerque, commander of the Portuguese fleet and governor of India. In 1510, when Diogo Mendes de Vascogoncellos was sent by the King of Portugual to help the hard-pressed Albuquerque reconquer Goa, he met a ship on which were two very rich Castilian Jews. Their destination was Cananor, and there Albuquerque became acquainted with them. In answer to his questions, they gave him detailed information concerning the kingdom of Prester John (who, they said, had a Jewish admiral in his service), and concerning the Arabian Gulf, the commerce of those regions, and various other matters. Albuquerque gave the two Spanish Jews many tokens of his esteem, and induced them to abandon Judaism, at least for a short time. One of them called himself Francisco d'Albuquerque, after his patron, whom he loyally

---

* Correa, *Lendas da India*, i. 656 sq., 900.

served as interpreter.* The other, whose real name was Cufo or Hucefe but who called himself Alexander d'Atayde, was a very experienced and trustworthy man, who knew many languages,† and hence Albuquerque appointed him his secretary. He became Albuquerque's adviser, his constant companion, and most intimate friend; and at the surrender of the stronghold of Ormuz he rendered his employer important services. He enjoyed the admiral's complete confidence; and when the latter, slandered by his enemies and discredited by his sovereign, died in Goa broken-hearted, Hucefe at King Manuel's request made a journey to Lisbon. He succeeded in giving the king a better opinion of the great hero and statesman who had been calumniated at the royal court.

In Lisbon Hucefe was in danger of being robbed of his property, which he always carried with him in the form of gold and precious stones;

---

* Albuquerque employed as interpreters other Jews who had been expelled from the Iberian Peninsula, for example, a certain Samuel of Cairo. Barros, *Asia*, dec. 2, lib. 7, cap. 8.

† ". . . . homem de muyta verdade e que sabia muytas lingoas, e muy sabido em todolas cousas, e muy verdadeiro, com que era muyto do conselho do Governador;" Correa, *Lendas da India*, ii. 134. "Hucefe . . . homem em que tinha muyta confiança, que era homem de muyto saber em todolas lingoas e nas cousas dos Mouros, e homem de muyto verdade, com que o Governador se muyto aconselhaue;" *Ibid.*, ii. 177.

but he found shelter in the house of Garcia de Noronha, Albuquerque's nephew, whose acquaintance he had made in India. Garcia received him hospitably and manifested his esteem for him in the presence of the nobility of Lisbon. He soon left Lisbon and started on his voyage back to India. He proceeded to Cairo, where he again openly professed Judaism.*

---

* Correa, ii. 135. " E morto Affonso Dalboquerque vieram se pera Portugal em tempo del Rey D. Manuel, e daqui tornáram a India e da India se foram ao Cairo e se tornáram Judeos ; " *Commentarios do grande Affonso Dalboquerque* [Lisbon, 1777], pp. 269 sq. According to Correa, ii. 177, Francisco d'Albuquerque died in Goa, leaving a family of several sons.

In 1528, when Lopo Vaz de Sampayo was governor of India, the Turks sent a fleet to help the King of Calicut ; its commander was called "the great Jew" (*o grã Judeu*). This Jew with his fleet also hastened to the assistance of Khair-ed-din Barbarossa, when the latter was attacked by the admiral Andreas Doria. *Documentos remittidos da India, publ. da Academia real das sciencias de Lisboa, p. R. Ant. de Bulhão Pato* [Lisbon, 1880], iii. 274.

" As to Coron, it was reported at Rome a few days ago that Andrea Doria was informed that the famous Jewish pirate had prepared a strong fleet to meet the Spanish galleys which are to join Dorias' nineteen." *Letters and Papers of the Reign of Henry VIII.*, vi. 427.

CHAPTER VIII.

COLUMBUS'S DOWNFALL—ROYAL FAVORS GRANTED TO LUIS DE SANTANGEL—DEATH OF SANTANGEL AND OF GABRIEL SANCHEZ; THEIR DESCENDANTS—EARLIEST SETTLEMENTS OF MARRANOS IN ESPAÑOLA AND IN THE PORTUGUESE COLONIES—THE INQUISITION AND ITS VICTIMS IN THE COLONIES.

THE reception which Columbus met with on his return to Spain after his second voyage was very different from that which had been accorded him in Barcelona three years earlier. The constant complaints concerning his avarice, arrogance, and cruelty had shattered his reputation. Queen Isabella, who ruthlessly ordered Jews and Moors to be burned, had instructed him to be kind and indulgent toward the Indians. But he treated the natives cruelly; he harassed them with fire and sword. By his domineering conduct he also aroused the enmity of Juan Rodriguez de Fonseca, mentioned in the preceding chapter, who afterwards became Bishop of Plasencia. In an outburst of anger he kicked and violently assailed the Marrano Ximeno of Briviesca, Fonseca's accountant. Hence Fonseca became the explorer's greatest enemy. By his arrogant and heartless conduct he also aroused the enmity of the ship-physician, the Marrano Maestre Bernal. The conspiracy of Porras in Jamaica fomented by Bernal and by a certain Camacho seriously affected the admiral's destiny.* Until his death, which took place on May 20, 1506, in Valladolid, the discoverer of the New World had to endure considerable ill-fortune. While in this distressing situation, he frequently asked his old patron Gabriel Sanchez to intercede with Ferdinand and Isabella in his behalf; he also turned frequently for help to Luis de Santangel, who had been his ardent supporter in the past.†

Owing to Santangel's unselfishness Ferdinand always remained his loyal friend, and bestowed upon him many distinguished tokens of gratitude, for his great services to the crown and state. It was out of regard for Santangel that equal rights were granted to the Aragonese and Castilians in the New World.‡ From his marriage with Juana, who belonged to the distinguished and widely-ramified Marrano family of De la Caballeria, Santangel had several sons and one daughter, Luisa. In the spring of 1493 Luisa married Angel de Villanueva, who was afterwards ap-

---

* Navarrete, *Coleccion de los Viages*, i. 348.
† *Ibid.*, i. 335.
‡ Cesáreo Fernández Duro, *Tradiciones infundadas* [Madrid, 1888].

pointed governor of the county of Cerdeña.* The king gave her a wedding present of thirty thousand sueldos, " in recognition of the many services which her father, the well-beloved councillor and *escribano de racion* of his household, had rendered and was still rendering him."† Envy on account of this mark of distinction disturbed the treasurer Gabriel Sanchez. He intimated to the king that his services to the crown and to the state were as great as Santangel's. Hence his son Pedro, on his marriage with Maria del Jjar, also received thirty thousand sueldos as a wedding gift.‡

The highest mark of distinction accorded to Luis de Santangel, " in reward of the many great and notable services which he had rendered the king with untiring zeal and with great promptness and solicitude," was a grant made by Ferdinand on May 30, 1497. This grant exempted him as well as his sons Fernando, Geronimo, and Alfonso, and his daughter Luisa, together with their children and heirs, from every charge of apostasy. In this document the crown also granted them the absolute possession of all personal and real

---

* He was a nephew of Moses Pazagon of Calatayud.

† See Appendix v.

‡ The document is dated Torre Villas, May 10, 1494. *Arch. de la Corona de Aragon*, Reg. 3616, fol. 215.

property which should fall to them, to their children, or to their heirs during their life-time or after their death, and which might be confiscated by the Church or the state on the ground of any accusation of apostasy. Finally, the servants of the Inquisition in Valencia and elsewhere were admonished, on pain of paying a large fine, not to molest them, their children, or their descendants.*

Luis de Santangel and Gabriel Sanchez died one year earlier than Columbus. After the demise of Sanchez, which occurred on September 15, 1505, the office of treasurer passed to his son Luis, who held it till his death on December 4, 1530. On January 30, 1506, Ferdinand appointed as Luis de Santangel's successors his son Fernando and his kinsman Jaime de Santangel; each was to have a salary of 8,000 sueldos and the customary perquisites. The appointments were confirmed on July 24, 1512.† Soon after the king's death, however, Fernando was deprived of his office, and Pedro Celdrán was appointed *escribano de racion*. Hence Fernando felt constrained to defend his rights before the *Justitia*, the supreme court of Aragon.‡

---

* See Appendix vi. † See Appendix vii.
‡ In 1506 he had received 3,600 sueldos for special services rendered to the crown. The document, dated Salamanca, January 8, 1506, is in *Arch. de la Corona de Aragon*, Reg. 3555, fol. 123.

At that time the jurist Luis de Santangel, who had been appointed deputy of the Zalmedina for the year 1492, with all the honors and rights attached to that position, was deputy of the *Justitia* of Aragon,* and Salvador de Santangel of Saragossa was councillor. † In 1517 the Aragonese tribunal decided in favor of Fernando.‡ With Miguel Luis de Santangel, who in 1586 was a distinguished teacher of law and an alderman of Saragossa, the Santangels disappear from the history of Spain. That country will always cherish and honor the memory of Luis de Santangel, the pride of that family and the prominent promoter of the discovery of America.

From the outset Columbus gave the newly discovered lands a decidedly religious or ecclesiastical coloring. They had been discovered for the glory of Christianity and for the propagation of Catholicism, and hence he desired that they should be inhabited exclusively by Catholics. Moors and

---

* See the document, dated Granada, November 26, 1491, in Appendix iv. "... Micer Luis de Santangel, lugarteniente del Justicia de Aragon ;" *Libro de Actos de Zaragoza.*

† *Libro de Actos de Zaragoza.*

‡ " Sentencia á favor de Fernando de Santangel escribano de racion cujo oficio le disputada Pedro Celdrán, anno 1517." *Arch. de la Corona de Aragon*, Reg. 3880, fol. 36.

Jews were not to be allowed to settle there; even the Marranos, including those who had been persecuted and punished by the Inquisition, were prohibited from migrating to the New World. Nevertheless, the first person who obtained the king's permission to carry on trade with the newly discovered lands was Juan Sanchez of Saragossa, a secret Jew, whose father's loyalty to his ancestral faith had cost him his life. He lived in Seville, and was a nephew of the treasurer Gabriel Sanchez; hence he was also frequently called "*Juan Sanchez de la Tesorería.*" In the year 1502 he received permission from Isabella to take five caravels loaded with wheat, barley, horses, and other wares to Española without paying duty.* Two years later, on November 17, 1504, when the queen was very ill in Medina del Campo, Ferdinand allowed him to export merchandise and other articles to Española, and to sell or exchange them for the products of that land. This favor was granted in return for certain "good services" which he had rendered the crown, and with the understand-

---

* "Capitulacion con Juan Sanchez de la Tesor^a por la R^a en Toledo, 12 Setembro, 1502: Tesor^a podra llevar 5 carav^{os} con 300 cab. de trigo é 100 de cevada, 6 cavallos . . . é mercaderias. Todo lo sacaron libra de derechos." *Coleccion Muñoz* (*Biblioteca de la real Academia de la Historia en Madrid*), vol. 75, fol. 143.

ing that such services were to continue in the future.*

In spite of the stringent laws prohibiting emigration, large numbers of Spanish and Portuguese fugitives from the infernal flames of the *autos-de-fe*—nobles, men of learning, physicians, and prosperous merchants—soon settled in Española and on the other islands of the Indies. They tilled the soil, carried on trade, promoted industry,† and filled public offices. Hence already in 1511 Queen Juana of Spain was obliged to adopt measures against the secret Jews, "the sons and grandsons of the burned," who held public offices. Every secret Jew who, without the permission of the crown, was in possession of such an office, was to lose it, and was, furthermore, to be punished with the confiscation of his property.‡ This

---

* "El Rey. Por hacer bien é merced á vos Juan Sanchez de la Tesorería, estante en la ciudad de Sevilla, natural de la ciudad de Zaragoza, natural del reino de Aragon, acatando algunos buenos servicios que me habeis fecho, é espero que me fareis de aqui adelante, por la presente vos doy licencia para que podais llevar á la isla Española ques en el mar océano las mercaderías é otras cosas . . . " Navarrete, *Coleccion de los Viages*, iii. 525; Navarrete, *Coleccion de Opusculos* [Madrid, 1848], i. 106.

† Jews expelled from Portugal first introduced the cultivation of sugar from the island of Madeira into America. Antonio de Capmany y de Montpalan, *Memorias historicas sobre la marina, comercio y artes de Barcelona* [Madrid, 1779], ii. 43.

‡ The decree is dated, October 5, 1511 ; see Appendix xviii.

decree also introduced the Spanish Inquisition into the newly discovered lands, and full scope was given to its nefarious activity. One of the first victims of the Holy Office in Española was Diego Caballero of Barrameda, whose mother and father (Juan Caballero), according to the statement of two witnesses, had been persecuted and condemned by the Inquisition in Spain.*

Many secret Jews from Spain and Portugal also soon settled in the Portuguese Indies, especially in Brazil. They were scattered along the whole coast of the Portuguese colonies, and carried on an extensive trade in precious stones with Venice, Turkey, and other countries.† As soon as they felt secure, they threw off the mask of dissimulation and openly professed Judaism. Hence it is not strange that, as in the mother-country—in Lisbon, Evora, and Coimbra—so also in Goa, the metropolis of the Portuguese dominion in India, the Inquisition was established, with jurisdiction over the Portuguese possessions in Asia and Africa as far as the Cape of Good Hope.

To prevent the emigration of Marranos to the Indies, the king, or rather the regent, Cardinal

---

* *Coleccion de Documentos inéditos rel. al descubrimiento, conquista y organizacion de las antiguas posesiones españoles. Segunda seria* [Madrid, 1885], i. 422.

† *Documentos remittidos da India*, iii. 495.

Enrique, issued an edict on June 30, 1567, which stringently prohibited them from leaving Portugal without the special permission of the crown; any Marrano, however, could leave the kingdom provided he found a surety for at least five hundred cruzados, which were to be forfeited to the state if he did not return within a year. As this law did not prevent the secret Jews from migrating to the Indies to escape the oppressions of the Holy Office, a similar but more stringent edict of March 15, 1568, decreed that persons infringing this enactment should lose all their property; onehalf was to be given to the informer, the other half to the state treasury.* Captains of ships received strict orders to imprison all Marranos found on any vessel sailing to the Indies, and to deliver them to the governor-general.† Not until the Jews and Marranos in the colonies offered to pay the state the enormous sum of 1,700,000 cruzados, was the prohibition to migrate rescinded by the law of May 21, 1577. This law allowed them freedom of residence and of trade; in the future, no one was to call them Jews, New Christians, or Marranos. ‡

---

* The law of March 15, 1568, is printed in *Documentos remittidos*, iii. 510 sq.

† *Ibid.*, ii. 215 sq.

‡ Porto Seguro (F. A. de Varnhagen), *Historia geral de Brasil*, 2d edition [Rio de Janeiro, n.d.], 412.

Notwithstanding the great sums of money which they paid for the right to reside in the colonies, the persecutions of the Inquisition continued, and hence the Jews in the Indies soon became a source of serious embarrassment to the Portuguese government. They made common cause with the Dutch, who were at that time fighting for freedom, and they gave them financial and other assistance. In their zealous love of freedom they even equipped ships expressly for the Dutch. A letter of King Philip II. to Martin Affonso de Castro, Viceroy of the Indies, states that two New Christians in Columbo were in active correspondence with the Dutch, and that four or five in Malacca were giving the latter definite information concerning the military plans of the Portuguese. The Marranos of the Indies sent considerable supplies to the Spanish and Portuguese Jews in Hamburg and Aleppo, who, in turn, forwarded them to Holland and Zealand.*

---

* " . . . . os Christãos-Novos de Portugal e Hispanha ajudavan a D. Manuel para armar alguns navios de guerra junto com os dos mercadores que por todos fizessen copia de trinta velas, e n'ellas ir D. Manuel para que mandavan dinheiro a Hamburgo e Alepo, e d'ahi se passava a Holanda e Gelanda, e que os Christãos-Novos d'esse Estado entravam tamben na dita liga, e que em Columbo havia dous que se carteavam com os Hollandeses, e em Malaca havia quatro ou cinco que os avisavam pelos moços que jam aos portos onde elles estavam por cuja via havia d'ahi muita correspondencia con ellas." *Documentos remittidos*, i. 106.

As soon as the Portuguese government heard of these transactions, the Viceroy of the Indies was ordered to adopt stringent measures against the New Christians who were thus allied with the Dutch. The law of March 15, 1568, was renewed, and the captains of ships received peremptory instructions to confiscate for the state treasury all the property of New Christians who should be found on their vessels, and to send them back to Portugal. If no ship happened to be ready to return to Portugal, these New Christians were to be carried to Goa, and were there to be retained in prison by the Inquisition until some ship set sail for the mother-country. The Inquisition was to deal in a similar manner with the Jews and New Christians who had already settled in the colonies; a number of them were to be sent back annually to Portugal, and thus the Indies were gradually to be purged.*

After the death of Cardinal Enrique in 1580, Philip II. of Spain, in his greed for new acquisitions of territory, also brought Portugal under his sway. Not merely was Portugal added to Spain, but the Eastern Indies were also united to the Western Indies; Asia as well as America fell under Philip II.'s dominion. Spain was now at the zenith of her power.

---

* *Doc. remittidos*, ii. 195 sq., iii. 7.

Philip II. was the son of a daughter of the Portuguese king, Dom Manuel, and he was a grandson of that handsome Philip whose infidelity caused the insanity of his wife Juana, a daughter of Isabella the Catholic. Under this melancholy, tyrannical monarch the Inquisition renewed its nefarious activity in America. Tribunals of the Holy Office were established in Peru and Lima, and Jews and Marranos were consigned to the flames.

Among the first victims of the Inquisition in Lima was the physician Juan Alvarez of Zafra; he was publicly burned as an adherent of Judaism, together with his wife and children and his nephew Alonso Alvarez. A few years later Manuel Lopez of Yelves in Portugal, also called Luis Coronado, met the same fate. He frankly confessed that he was a Jew, and he made no attempt to conceal the fact that he and his co-religionists had observed the Mosaic law and had held religious services in his house. Duarte Nuñez de Cea, a merchant forty-one years of age, also died for his religion. Before ascending the funeral pyre he confessed that as a Jew he had lived, observing the precepts of Judaism, and that it was his simple wish to die a Jew, as his ancestors had done. His example of religious loyalty was followed by the learned physician

Alvaro Nuñez of Braganza, who lived in La Plata, and by Diego Nuñez de Silva and Diego Rodriguez de Silveyra of Peru. New-comers from Portugal were persecuted with particular rigor. On one day fourteen such immigrants were arrested at the king's command, and their property was confiscated.* In the case of King Philip and his successors on the Spanish throne— as in the case of their ancestors Ferdinand and Isabella—fanaticism had its root in the material interests of the state.

In spite of such persecutions thousands of secret Jews fled, during the sixteenth and seventeenth centuries, from the Iberian Peninsula to the Indies, and especially to America—to the New World, which was not merely a land rich in gold and silver mines, but also the land where the light of freedom first shone upon the adherents of Judaism.

---

* J. T. Medina, *Historia del Tribunal del S. Oficio de la Inquisicion de Lima* [Santiago, 1887].

APPENDIX.

I.

FERDINAND I. OF ARAGON GRANTS PRIVILEGES TO THE SANTANGELS (1415.)

[*Arch. de la Corona de Aragon,** *Reg.* 2391, *fol.* 28.]

FERDINANDUS . . . Delectis et fidelibus universis et singulis officialibus nostris presentibus et futuris vel eorum locumtenentibus ad quos infrascripta pertinere noscantur salutem et deleccionem.

Cum Magister Alfonsus de Santangel, Johannes Martinus de Santangel, Petrus Martinus de Santangel, vicini ciuitatis Daroce, judaycis cecitatibus postergatis obumbrati spiritus sancti gracia ad Catholice fidei claritatem et cultum de proximo sint conversi ideo nostris mereantur precipue rationalibus adque justis fauoribus confoueri nec sic justicia prout ante caligine ofuscatos judayca pertractari vobis et unicumque vestrum dicimus et mandamus de nostri certa sciencia quatenus non obstantibus quibusuis elongamentis sub quacumque forma concessis que huic possent quomodolibet obuiare in bonis eorum aut cujusuis ipsorum qui in dictis tam nominibus propriis quam donacionem per Xpianos vel Judeos sibi factarum obnoxii et obligati extiterint juxta formam contractuum seu instrumentorum super debitis censualibus seu commandis inde factorum seu firmatorum pro omnibus et singulis dictis debitis censualibus et commandis prout sua debita justicia usuris tamen inde debitis seu percipiendis exceptis quo ad quos volumus elongamenta ipsa in suis viribus permanere excepcionem promptam et

---

* In Barcelona.

rigidam faciatis quibusuis excepcione, consultacione, delacione et dubio friuolis ultrajectis : hocque non mutetis seu etiam differatis aliqua racione cum nos justicie mediant seu fieri prouiderimus et velimus. Cauentes attente ne dicti Magister Alfonsus de Santangel, Johannes Martinus de Santangel et Petrus Martinus de Santangel aut aliquis eorum pro predictis vestri ob culpam videantur coram nobis aliquatenus conquerentes non culpa vestra ipsa vero carebat sine dubio digna pena.

Datum Perpiniani sub nostro sigillo secreto XXIII die octobris anno a Nativitate Dom. M°CCCCXV°.

Et propter indisposicionem nostre persone signatum manu nostri primogeniti

A. Primogenitus.

Dominus rex mandavit mihi Paulo Nicholae.

II.

Juan II. of Aragon Allows the Santangels to Search for Treasures (1459).

[*Arch. de la Corona de Aragon, Reg.* 3368, *fol.* 77.]

Johannes Rex . . . Delectis fidelibus nostris Bajulo et Vicario Calatayubii et ejus locumtenentibus et ceteris quibusuis officialibus et subditis nostris ad quem seu quos presentes peruenerint et fuerint presentate salutem et graciam.

Pro parte fidelis nostri Ludouici de Sancto Angelo jurisperiti minoris dierum ciuis Cesarauguste fuit Majestati nostre expositum reuerenter quod ipse et Leonardus de Sancto Angelo ciuis Calatayubii quasdam domos in vico seu partita vocata Villanueva que confrontantur cum domibus que fuerunt Ferdinandi Lupi de Villanueva et cum domibus que fuerunt Ludouici Sanchez de Calatayud et cum torrente siue barranco et cum via publica ex alia parte

quasquidem domus habuerunt in successione parentum et
auorum suorum et in quibus quidem domibus ut fertur aui
uel parentes eorum recondiderunt in aliquibus partibus
dictarum domorum pecunias, monetas, auri uel argenti et
nonnulla bona per eos ibidem occultata et facilius pro eis
qui tempore mortis eorum parentum remanebant pupilli et
in valde parua aetate conseruarentur ut predicta demon-
strantur ut fertur per memorialia priuata manu aui et sui
patris eorum scripta quas quidem domus dicti Ludouicus
et Leonardus vendiderunt Abrahe Patagon judeo dicti
ciuitatis Calatayubii seu pro eo Raymundo Lopez ejus fratri
retento sibi quod possent quotiens eis placeret dictas domus
perquirere et quod ibidem reperirent inde libere asportare.
Et quamuis illud possint libere facere et maxime cum dictus
judeus qui dictas domus detinet in dicta voluntate et pacto
perseueret, tamen ut illa facilius et absque aliquo scrupulo
et metu nostro seu fisci nostri fieri valiant supplicauit nobis
dictus Ludouicus quod sibi licenciam et facultatem per-
quirendi et fodiendi in dictis domibus dictas pecunias,
monetas et bona et quidquid aliud ibi perquirere uellet
concedere dignaremus et quod quidquid ibidem inuenerit
possit et valeat secum apportare et inde ad suas uoluntates
facere offerens se seruire Majestati nostre de quinta parte
illorum que ibidem repererit. Idcirco ad dicti Ludouici
supplicacionem ac considerantes quod supplicata per eum
rationi et justicie sunt consona, idcirco tenore presentis
prouisionis nostre perpetue valiture concessimus et concedimus liberam facultatem permissam et licenciam dicto
Ludouico quod precedente assensu et voluntate dicti
Abrahe Patagon habitantis in dictis domibus expensis
tamen dicti Ludouici possit et valeat tociens quociens sibi
uisum fuerit ipse per se aut alios in dictis domibus et quali-
bet partita earum fodere, perquirere et quouismodo inda-
gare presente tamen vobis dicto bajulo aut vestro locum-
tenenti aut alia persona a vobis aut altero vestrum deputata
seu deputanda et quidquid ibidem inuenerit aut repererit

retenta apud vos quinta parte pro nobis et erario nostro possit libere totum residuum accipere et inde extrare et secum asportare et inde ad suas voluntates ut de bonis propriis facere absque aliquo metu, pena aut calonia et absque alicujus impedimento. Uolumus tamen quod dictus Ludouicus in posse vestro aut vestri locumtenentis promittat et assecuret quod quidquid in dictis domibus foderit, demolitus fuerit aut innouauerit, restituet in primerum statum suis expensis propriis. Mandantes vobis et cuilibet vestrum ceterisque quibusuis officialibus et subditis nostris quatenus dictam nostram licenciam et facultatem firmas teneant et obseruent, teneri et obseruari faciant et quod contra ea non veniant, faciant aut uenire permittant, ymo dicto Ludouico in predictis foueant et non contraueniant aliqua occasione seu causa cum nos deliberate et consulte ita fieri decreuerimus et velimus.

Datum in nostra Aliaferia ciuitatis Ceserauguste die XXIIII mensis octobris anno a Natuitate Dom. M°CCCC°LVIIII°.

Rex Jo.

Dominus Rex mandauit mihi Antonio Nogueras et viderunt eam Generalis Thesaurarius et Petrus Torrellas Conseruator Aragonum.

III.

FERDINAND THE CATHOLIC GRANTS A PENSION TO THE DAUGHTERS OF JUAN DE SANTANGEL (1488, 1492).

[*Arch. de la Corona de Aragon, Reg.* 3649, *fol.* 236 *sq.*]

NOS FERDINANDUS REX. . . . Fuit superioribus diebus Joannes de Sancto Angelo juris peritus ac ciuis ciuitatis Ceserauguste per deuotos patres inquisitores heretice prauitatis in eadem ciuitate ob crimen heresis et apostasie de quo fuit accusatus in absencia comdemnatus ac ejus effigies siue statua igni tradita et combusta bonaque sua omnia mobilia et immobilia censualia jura nomina et acciones preuia racione Curie et fisco nostris adjudicata, confiscata et applicata prefati inquisitores sua cum sentencia declararunt prout in eadem sentencia quam hic pro sufficienter specificata, repetita et inserta haberi volumus, et habemus proinde ac si de verbo ad verbum hic expressa, repetita et inserta foret predicta confiscacio et alia lacius et effusius sunt expressa. Post quam condemnacionem et bonorum confiscacionem quoniam intelleximus dictum Joannem tres filias reliquisse innuptas, vos scilicet Luisam, Agnetem et Lauram de Sancto Angelo que antea ex bonis ejusdem patris vestri vivebatis et quod eis manus ad vestras apprehensis nihil vobis pro sustentacione vite vestre remansit, nostra cum prouisione data Ceseraguste decimo nono januarii anni Millesimi quadringentesimi octogesimi octaui fecimus vobis graciam et concessionem de mille et quingentis solidis jaccensibus per vos annis singulis vestra durante vita recipiendis ac inter vos certo modo diuidendis quos vobis dari et assignari jussimus in quibuscumque censualibus et redditibus Curie nostre confiscatis qui et que fuerunt dicti vestri genitoris ut in precalendata nostra prouisione ad quam nos refferimus hoc et alia lacius vidimus contineri cujus concessiones vigore fuerunt ut intelleximus per receptorem nostrum bonorum videlicet confiscatorum ob crimen heresis in diocesi Ceseraguste vobis assignati dicti mille et quingenti solidi jaccenses annuales super quoddam censuali onerato et carricato in et super consiliis Universitatis et singularibus personis locorum honoris de Huesca pensionis annue mille solidorum ad censum soluendorum singulis annis primo die februarii et precii siue proprietatis quindecim mille solidorum et super alio censuali onerato et carricato in et super Aljama judeorum Ciuitatis Jacce et singularibus ejusdem pensionis annue quingentorum solidorum jaccensium annis singulis soluendorum primo die februarii et precii siue proprietatis sex mille solidorum jaccensium que duo censualia fuerunt dicti patris vestri et pretextu dicte confiscacionis Curie et fisco nostris adquisita et applicata ac ea vos in presenciam modo predicto tenetis et possidetis. Et quoniam ut intelleximus ob bonorum indigenciam nubere non voletis, fuit propterea vestra pro parte Majestati nostre humiliter supplicatum et premencionata duo censualia tam in proprietatibus quam pensionibus in adjutorium matrimonii vobis tribus in perpetuum concedere pro vobis et successoribus vestris de nostra solita clemencia dignaremur. Nos vero quia opus caritatis hoc esse perspicimus predictisque et aliis piis moti respectibus eadem supplicacione benigne exaudita tenore presentis Carte nostre cunctis futuris temporibus perpetuo valiture scienter deliberate et consulto per nos omnes que heredes et successores nostros quoscumque donacione quidem pura, perfecta et irrevocabilique dicitur inter uiuos damus, donamus, concedimus et liberaliter vobis predictis Luyse, Agneti et Laure sororibus inter vos modo infrascripto diuidenda et vestris et quibus volueritis perpetuo premencionata duo censualia tam in preciis siue in proprietatibus quam in pensionibus illorum et utriusque eorum ab inde debendis seu decurrendis cum penis salariis et aliis clausulis obligacionibus et firmitatibus in instrumentis eorumdem censualium et illorum sentenciis super eis latis lacius contentis et expressis videlicet predictum censuale pensionis annue mille solid. jaccens. et precii siue proprietatis quindecim mille solid. jaccens. pro vobis dicta Laura et vestris et quibus volueritis perpetuo et expedito altero censuali pensionis annue quingentorum solidorum et precii siue proprietatis sex mille solid. jaccens. due partes videlicet trecenti triginta tres solidi quatuor denarii dicte pensionis cum eorum precio siue proprietate pro vobis dicta Agnete et vestris et quibus volueritis perpetuo et tertia pars que est centum sexaginta sex solidi octo denarii restantes dicti pensionis quingentorum solidorum cum eorum precio siue proprietate pro vobis dicta Agnete et vestris et quibus volueritis perpetuo. Et tertia pars que est centum sexaginta sex solidi octo denarii restantes dicte pensionis quingentorum solid. cum eorum precio siue proprietate pro vobis dicta Luysa vestra vita durante et post vestram vitam volumus quod vos dicta Agnes succedatis in dictis centum sexaginta sex solidis octo denariis pensionis et in eorum precio siue proprietate de quibus dicto in casu nunc pro tunc et contra vobis graciam et donacionem facimus. Ita quod de eis predicto in casu possitis disponere in vos et vestros in perpetuum ad vestre libitum voluntatis quemadmodum hujusmodi nostre donacionis pretextu vobis licet disponere de aliis duabus partibus dicti censualis tam in proprietate quam in pensionibus de quibus ut prefertur vobis graciam et donacionem facimus, sed si et ubi continget dictum censuale pensionis annue quingentorum solidorum et precii siue proprietatis sex mille solidorum jaccens. reducti seu quitari siue uiuente dicta Luysa siue post ejus obitum volumus quod totum precium seu proprietas ejusdem censualis sit vestre dicte Agnetis ac vobis pertineat vosque de eadem proprietate possitis in vos et vestros disponere in perpetuum ad vestre libitum voluntatis. Eo tamen pacte et condicione quod teneamini et obligate sitis et vestri in dicto censuali seu in precio illius successores suo casu teneantur et obligati existant respondere et realiter et cum effectu soluere racione dicti censualis predicte Luyse singulis annis ejus vita durante dictos sexaginta sex solidos octo denarios jaccens. qui post ipsius obitum dicte Agneti integre remaneant ut predicitur. Hanc autem donacionem et ex causa donacionis concessionem facere intendimus et facimus vobis dictis Laure, Agneti et Luyse sororibus singula singulis refferendo prout superius est expressum et vestris et quibus volueritis perpetuo ut prefertur sicut melius plenius, sanius et utilius dici potest et intelligi ad sanum, sincerum et bonum etiam intellectum vestri et vestrorum predictorum. Extrahentes predicta que vobis damus, donamus et concedimus a jure dominio posse proprietate nostri et nostrorum eademque omnia et singula in vos vestrumque ac vestrorum jus dominium proprietatem et potestatem mittimus, ponimus et transferimus irreuocabiliter pleno jure ad habendum, tenendum omnique tempore pacifice et perpetuo possidendum et inde vestras vestrorumque uoluntates omnino ad libere faciendum sine obstaculo, contradictione et impedimento nostri et nostrorum et alterius cujuscumque Curie et persone promittentes tradere vobis et cuilibet vestrum aut cui seu quibus volueritis loco vestri possessionem corporalem seu quasi predictorum que vobis ut prefertur donamus et in ea facere vos et vestros existere perpetuo pociores vel vos et vestri si malueritis, possitis et valeatis dictam possessionem libere apprehendere quandocumque volueritis penes vos et eos licite retinere. Nos enim interim donec possessionem ipsam vobis tradiderimus vel vos aut vestri predictam apprehenderitis ut est dictum fatemur et confitemur nos predicta que vobis damus, concedimus et donamus pro vobis et vestris vestroque et ipsorum nomine tenere et possidere vel quasi scientes illum de jure possidere cujus nomine possidetur. Preterea ex causa hujusmodi donacionis et concessionis et alias prout melius de jure valere poterit et tenere, damus, cedimus et mandamus vobis et vestris predictis omnia jura et loca nostra omnesque voces et vices, raciones et actiones reales et personales utiles, mixtas et directas, ordinarias et extraordinarias et alias. Nos enim facimus et constituimus vos et vestros predictos in his dominos et procuratores, ut in rem vestram et eorum propriam ad faciendum inde vestre libitum voluntatis dicentes nihilominus et intimantes tenore presentis Carte nostre vicem epistole in hac parte gerentis dictis conciliis Xpianorum et Aljame judeorum et aliis singularibus personis tentis et obligatis in predictis censualibus et quolibet eorum seu que ab inde tenebuntur quauis racione vel causa quadammodo habeant et teneant vos et vestros predictos et quos volueritis predominis dictorum censualium tam in proprietatibus quam in pensionibus vobis et cuilibet vestrum aut cui seu quibus volueritis respondeant et satisfaciant de pro ratis et pensionibus ab inde debendis et ut predicitur de preciis eorundem censualium prout virtute precalendate concessionis nostre et assignacionis predicte per receptorem ejus pretextu facte vobis durante vita vestra de dictis pensionibus et post vestri obitum nobis et successoribus nostris de pensionibus et preciis respondere et satisfacere tenebantur ante hujusmodi donacionem, concessionem et cessionem. Hanc autem donacionem et concessionem dictorum censualium dictis sororibus facimus et facere intendimus cum his pacto et condicione et non alias neque alio modo quod nullo unquam tempore possitis neque valeatis aliquid aliud de bonis et hereditate dicti Joannis de Sancto Angelo genitoris vestri habere, exigere seu quomodolibet petere sed de dictis et premencionatis duobus censualibus contente sitis atque satisfacte pro omnibus et singulis juribus et accionibus in bonis et hereditate dicti patris vestri vobis pertinentibus et expectantibus. Illustrissimo propterea Joanni principi Asturiarum et Gerunde primogenito nostro carissimo ac in omnibus regnis et terris nostris post felices et longeuos dies nostros immediato heredi dicimus magnificis vero consiliariis delectis et fidelibus nostris regenti officium nostri emolumentorum et bonorum Curie et fisco nostris confiscatorum ex causa heresis et apostasie criminum predictorum nec non Çalmedine, merinis, justiciis, alguziriis supra juntariis, nunciis et sagionibus et aliis uniuersis et singulis officialibus et subditis nostris in regno ipso Aragonum constitutis, constituendis dictorumque officialium locumtenentibus ceterisque uniuersis et singulis personis ad quos spectat et presertim predictis conciliis Aljame et aliis singularibus personis que ad prestacionem dictorum censualium tenentur et obligateque sunt et de cetero fuerunt dicimus, precipimus et mandamus ad obtentum nostri amoris et gracie incursumque pene florenorum auri duorum mille nostris si contrafecerint inferendorum erariis quod renunciando vos dicte sorores omnibus juribus et accionibus quacumque racione seu causa vobis pertinentibus et spectantibus in bonis que fuerunt dicti patris vestri. Et dictus illustr. filius noster carissimus benediccionem nostram paternam caram habeat ceterique officiales nostri predicti iram et indignacionem ac penam prepositam cupiant non subire. In cujus rei testimonium presentem cartam fieri jussimus nostro communi sigillo impendenti munitam.

Datum in Ciuitate nostra Granate die VIII mensis Januarii anno a Nativitate Dom. M°CCCC°LXXXXII° Regnorum nostrorum videlicet Sicilie anno XXV° Castelle et Legionis XVIIII° Aragonum vero et aliorum XIIII°, Granate autem primo.

Yo el Rey F.

Testes sunt: R^{mus} ps. Cardinalius Archiepiscopus Toletanus.

Dominus Rex mandauit mihi Johanni de Coloma. Visa per generalem thesaurarium J. de la Caualleria.

IV.

Louis de Santangel is Appointed Deputy of the Zalmedina (1491).

[Libro de Act. del Ayuntamiento de Zaragoza, A° 1492.]

Nos Ferdinandus Rex . . . De fide legalitate et animi probitate viri delecti nostri Ludouici de Santangelo notari ciuitatis de Cesarauguste plenarii confidentes supplicacionibusque quarundam familiarum et benemeritorum nostrorum benigniter inclinati, Tenore presentis scienter et expresse officium Locumtenentis Çalmedine ac Judicis mynorum causarum pro anno proximo venturo nonagesimo segundo quod currere incipiet vespere conceptionis Beate Virginis Marie mensis Decembris proxime instantis et finiet eodem die anni jamdicti nonagesimi segundi cum salario jurisdictione preheminencio superjoritatibus utilitatibus honoribusque et oneribus officio ipsi incumbentibus debitis pertinentibus et spectantibus vobis dicto Ludouico de Santangelo prestito prius per vos in posse illius ad quem spectet debito et solito prestari juramento concedimus, committimus et fiducialiter commendamus. Itaque vos dictus Ludouicus de Santangelo et alius nemo dicto anno durante sitis Locumtenens Çalmedine ac Judex mynorum causarum ipsumque officium habeatis, teneatis, regatis et exerceatis fideliter legaliter atque bene dicto anno durante Jus et Justitia dicto submissis officio imbuendo et ministrando jura et regalias nostras manutenendo et conseruando et alia fauendo adque juxta ordinaciones, privilegia, statuta, obseruancias et consuetudines dicte civitatis teneamini et sitis astricti. Et habeatis, exigatis et recipiatis vestrisque utilitatibus applicetis pro labore et exercitio memorati illud salarium eove lucro jura obuenciones et emolumenta que per alios locumtenentes Çalmedine ac Judicis mynorum causarum predecessores vestros juste et debite sunt haberi et exigi solitum et solita. Mandantes per hanc eandem regenti officium gubernationis, justitie et Bajulo generali Aragonum, Çalmedine, Merino, Juratis et aliis officialibus et personis in dictis civitate et regno constitutis et eorum Locumtenentibus quatenus vos dictum Ludouicum de Santangelo teneant, reputent, honorificent atque tractent, et in possessione dicti officii ii eorum ad quos attineat adueniente tempore oportuno vos ponant et judicent positumque et inductum manteneant et conseruent respondeantque vobis et respondere faciant per quos deceat de salario, emolumentis et aliis juribus ratione dicti officii pertinentibus et vobis spectantibus, provisionemque nostram hujusmodi et omnia et singula desuper contenta ad unguem teneant et inuiolabiter obseruent et faciant per quos deceat obseruari. Et non contrafaciant uel veniant aut aliquem contrafacere sine ratione aliqua siue causa. In quorum testimonium presentem fieri jussimus nostro communi sigillo atergo munitam.

Datum in nostris felicibus castris agr. Ciuitatis Granate XXVI die Nouembris anno a Natiuitate Dom. Millesimo quadringentesimo nonagesimo primo.

Yo el Rey F.

V.

Luis de Santangel's Daughter Receives a Wedding Gift from Ferdinand the Catholic (1493).

[*Arch. de la Corona de Aragon, Reg.* 3616, *fol.* 207.]

D. Fernando . . . Al magnifico amado criado consejero y general thesorero nostro Gabriel Sanchez salud e dileccion.

Por los muchos seruicios que hauemos recebido y de cado dia recebimos del amado criado consejero y scriuano de racion de nostra casa M. Luys de Santangel en alguna compensa de aquellos, y por beneficios y honras a donna Luysa de Santangel su fija, la qual de voluntad y consentimiento nostro ha contractado matrimonio con el noble D. Angel de Villanueva, es nostra voluntad fazer le la merced en esta scripta. Dezimos, encargamos y mandamos vos que de qualesquiere pecunias de nostra Corte a vuestras manos peruenidas o que primero peruendran, deys y pageys realmente y de fecho a la dicha donna Luysa de Santangel o al dicho nostro Luys de Santangel su padre en su nombre o a quien su padre tuuiese treynta mil sueldos monedos de Valencia, de los quales lo hauemos fecho merced segund que conta presente le facemos por contemplacio del dicho su matrimonio.

Datum en la villa de Medina del Campo a XXI del mes del Marcio anyo de la natiuidad de n. S. MºCCCCºLXXXXIIIº.

Yo el Rey F.

VI.

GRANT OF FERDINAND THE CATHOLIC TO LUIS DE SANT-
ANGEL AND HIS DESCENDANTS: THEY ARE NOT TO BE
MOLESTED BY THE HOLY OFFICE (1497).

[*Arch. de la Corona de Aragon, Reg.* 3654, *fol.* 72 *sq.*]

JESU CRISTI nomine. Nouerint uniuersi quod Nos Ferdinandus Dei gracia Rex. . . Dignum profecto et consonum racioni esse arbitramur ut illos regalis clemencia congruis beneficiis prosequatur quos virtutis constancie fidelitatis et animi integritatis merita nostra munificencia et liberalitate reddiderunt benemeritos. Nam et ipsi de laboribus susceptis seruiciisque impensis senciunt retribucionem et ceteri ad similia peragenda ardenciori desiderio attenduntur: Considerantes itaque seruicia grandia et assidua et memoratu digna que vos magnificus dilectusque consiliarius et scriba porcionis Domus nostre Ludouicus de Sancto Angelo nobis prestitis animo quippe indefesso non sine maxima diligencia, cura, sollicitudine et vigilancia merito nos inducunt ut non modo in vos verum etiam in filios et posteritatem vestram nostram ostendamus munificenciam et liberalitatem in aliqualem igitur tantorum seruiciorum vestrorum recompensam longe majora de nobis promerencium tenore presentis carte nostre cunctis futuris temporibus firmiter valiture et durature per Nos et omnes heredes et successores nostros damus, donamus, concedimus et liberaliter elargimur nunc pro tunc et e contra Ferdinando de Sancto Angelo, Hieronimo et Alfonso filiis ac Luyse de Sancto Angelo filie vestri dicti Ludouici de Sancto Angelo et suis heredibus et successoribus et quibus voluerint omnes et quoscumque redditus, census, censualia, jura, acciones, prouentus et alia bona quecumque mobilia et immobilia ac se mouencia cujuscumque generis aut speciei sint qui uelque quomodocumque uel qualitercumque fuissent forte vobis vivente aut post vestri obitum racione criminis heresis et apostasie donacione quidem pura, perfecta et irreuocabili que dicitur inter viuos ad dandum, vendendum, alienandum, cedendum, transferendum, transportandum, tenendumque et perpetuo possidendum et inde in predictis censibus, bonis, juribus, redditibus, prouentibus et aliis quibuscumque bonis racione et ex causis predictis nobis et Curie ac fisco nostro pertinentibus et expectantibus, adjudicatis, adquisitis, applicatis et confiscatis seu adjudicandis, applicandis et confiscandis suas et suorum omnimodas uoluntates libere faciendum tanquam de re ut in rem suam et suorum propriam et dictis filiis vestris siue liberis descendentibus transeat et succedat ad illum heredem quem ultimus dictorum filiorum uestrorum suo ultimo testamento aut alias elegerit et nominauerit taliter quod presens nostra donacio in dictos filios et heredes vestros et in suos successores sicut ut premittitur de corpore vestro legitimo descendentes de uno ad alium transeat et in eos succedat ac in jus defuncti quicumque heres uti supra dicitur nominandus in presenti nostra donacione sit comprehensus etiam in eadem fuisset specialiter et expresse nominatus, contentus et operatus. Cedentes et transferentes hujusmodi serie dictis filiis et heredibus uestris et in eos et alios ut premittitur eis succedentes omnia jura et acciones nostras omnesque voces et vices nostros et nostrorum successorum reales et personales, mixtas, utiles et directas, ordinarias et extraordinarias et alias quascumque que nobis et successoribus nostris seu Curie et fisco nostro competunt aut in futurum quomodolibet competere poterunt quacumque racione uel causa. Hanc autem donacionem et ex causa donacionis cessionem et transportacionem de dictis bonis racione predicta nobis et successoribus nostris forte pertinentibus et que pertinere possent in futurum facimus prefatis filiis et heredibus vestris et suis ut premittitur successoribus, prout melius, sanius, comodius, plenius et utilius dici, scribi, annotari et intelligi potest ad suum et suorum bonum, sanum et sincerum intellectum ad habendum, tenendum omnique tempore pacifice possidendum indeque suas et suorum omnimodas voluntates libere de eisdem faciendum sine obstaculo uel impedimento nostri aut quorumcumque officialium nostrorum. Extrahentes predictis que dictis filiis et heredibus vestris et suis ut premittitur heredibus et successoribus damus et donamus a jure, posse, dominio et proprietate nostri et nostrorum eademque omnia in jus, posse, dominium et proprietatem suam et suorum ponimus, mittimus et transferimus irreuocabiliter pleno jure inducentes nunc pro tunc et e conuerso predictos filios et heredes vestros et suos heredes et successores in possessionem corporalem seu quasi realemque et actualem predictorum bonorum et jurium nobis pertinencium seuque in futurum possent quomodolibet nobis et nostris successoribus pertinere. Dantes et concedentes eisdem licenciam et facultatem plenarias predicta bona et eorum possessionem apprehendere et apprehensam penes eos licite retineri. Constituentes predictos filios et heredes vestros et suos in his successores vestros et potentes dominos, actores et procuratores ut in rem suam et eorum propriam. Nos enim licet bona ipsa fuerint ut premittitur racione predicta confiscata et adjudicata Regio fisco et Curie nostre confitemur predicta omnia predictis filiis et heredibus vestris et eorum successoribus precario nomine tenere et possidere scientes illum de jure possidere cujus nomine possidetur. Et ne in futurum in presenti nostra donacione, priuilegio siue carta defectu alicujus solemnitatis vel ommissionis clausule seu clausularum aliquod dubium possit suboriri seu defectus aliquis annotari uel ob eam rem de inualiditate uel nullitate argui seu impugnari ad omnem dubitacionem tollendam motu nostro proprio scienter deliberate et consulto hujusmodi tenore, ex nostre regie potestatis plenitudine legibus absoluta qua uti volumus in hac parte. Supplemus omnes et quoscumque defectus et solemnitatum ommissiones tam juris quam facti signi uelque in premissis aut aliqua premissorum occasione predicta aut alias suboriri possit seu quomodolibet annotari quibus non obstantibus uolumus presentem nostram donacionem juriumque et accionum nostrarum cessionemque et transportacionem suum debitum sortiri effectum et omnimodo obtinere roboris firmitatem quo circa Illmo Joanni principi Asturiarum et Gerunde primogenito nostro carissimo et post felices et longeuos dies nostros in omnibus regnis et terris nostris Deo propicio immediato heredi et successori nostro sub paternis benediccionibus obtineri dicimus et injungimus receptori quoque siue receptoribus bonorum propter crimen heresis et apostasie nobis et Curie nostre confiscatorum et confiscandorum presentibus pariter et futuris nec non etiam fisco siue fiscis nostris et judicibus siue commissariis bonorum confiscatorum siue confiscandorum in Ciuitate et Regno Valencie ac alibi creatorum et creandorum ceterisque demum uniuersis et singulis officialibus et judicibus dicte Inquisicionis et nostris in predictis Ciuitate et Regno ac alibi constitutis et constituendis et eorum locumtenentibus ad quos attineat dicimus, precipimus et jubemus scienter et expresse sub ire et indignacionis nostre incursu penaque florenorum auri Aragonum quinque millium a bonis cujuslibet contrafacientis irremissibiliter exigendorum et nostris inferendorum erariis quatenus presentem nostram donacionem juriumque et accionum nostrarum cessionem et transportacionem modo quo premittitur dictis filiis et heredibus vestris et suis factam teneant firmiter et obseruent, exequantur et compleant et dictis vestris filiis et heredibus in predictis foueant tenerique obseruari exequique et compleri ab omnibus faciant et in predictis nullum obstaculum aut impedimentum eis faciant aut fieri per aliquem permittant aliqua racione, occasione uel causa cum ita premissis respectibus et consideracionibus de mente nostra procedat ac per eos et eorum quolibet omnino compleri et fieri volumus omni dilacione et excusacione cessantibus. In quorum testimonium presentem fieri jussimus nostro communi sigillo impendente munitam.

Datum in Villa de Medina del Campo tricesimo die mensis Maii anno a Natiuitate Dom. M°CCCC° nonagesimo septimo regnorumque nostrorum videlicet Sicilie anno tricesimo Castelle et Legionis vicesimo quarto Aragonum et aliorum decimo, Granate autem sexto.

Yo el Rey F.

VII.

Jaime and Fernando de Santangel Receive Offices in the Royal Household (1506, 1512).

[*Arch. de la Corona de Aragon, Reg.* 3559, *fol.* 77 *sq.*]

Nos Ferdinandus Rex . . . . Recolimus quod nostro cum opportuno priuilegio debitis solemnitatibus expedito dato in Ciuitate Salamantice die tricesimo mensis januarii anni a Natiuitate Domini millesimi quingentesimi sexti prouidimus de officio Scribe porcionis domus nostre vobis magnifico dilecto consiliario nostro Jacobo de Santangelo conseruatori nostri regii patrimonii et Ferdinando de Santangelo militibus simul et in solidum vita vestra et ejus durante cum omnibus et singulis salario, graciis et accionibus, lucris et emolumentis cum omnibus et singulis honoribus, fauoribus, preheminenciis, prerogatiuis et prioritatibus aliisque ad dictum officium pertinentibus et spectantibus prout in dicto priuilegio lacius continetur. Et quia scienti fidedignorum testimonio percepimus solitum est et de more regie domus Aragonum quod Scriba porcionis nostre regie domus habere et recipere debet anno quolibet octo mille solidos barchinonenses pro assignacione et gracia officii jam dicti ultra salarium seu quitacionem ordinariam et assuetam et intencionis nostre sit ordinaciones et mores antiquas dicte domus ut decet conseruare presertim vobis dicto Jacobo de Santangelo qui tantumdem de nobis pro vestris seruiciis meriti estis quantum potuerunt Scribe porcionis quicumque de Serenissimis Regibus predecessoribus nostri mereri etiam si essetis his cui assignacio ipsa primo facta extitisset, quocirca presencium tenore expresse et de nostra certa sciencia et consulto octo mille solidos barchinonenses vobis dicto Jacobo de Santangelo Scribe porcionis predicto duximus assignandos et concedendos prout harum serie concedimus et assignamus ultra salarium siue quitacionem ordinariam ac assuetam memorati officii habendos siquidem exigendos et recipiendos annis singulis per vos eundem Jacobum de Santangelo vel procuratorem vestrum aut aliam legitimam personam tantum eum sic de mente nostra procedat certis bonis respectibus animum nostrum digne monentibus videlicet a die vicesimo octauo mensis augusti anni millesimi quingentesimi quinti antea et sic deinde annis singulis vita vestra durante in dicto uel consimili termino siue die exoluendos, dandos et tradendos vobis Jacobo de Santangelo aut procuratori vestro tantum realiter integre et cum effectu per generalem thesaurarium nostrum qui nunc est et pro tempore fuerit et de quibusuis redditibus, emolumentis et juribus ac pecuniis nostris seu Curie nostre ad ejus manus quomodolibet prouenientibus et prouenturis et in solucionibus quas de eis vobis facient legitimo procuratore tantummodo apochas desoluto in quantum prima tenor hujusmodi inseratur et in aliis solummodo mencionetur. In quorum testimonium presentem fieri jussimus nostro communi sigillo impendenti munitam.

Datum in Civitate Burgorum XXIIII mensis julii anno a Natiuitate Dom. Mill° quingent° duodecimo Regnorumque nostrorum uidelicet Sicilie vltra Farum a° quadrages° quinto Aragonum et aliorum quarto, Sicilie autem citra Farum et Hierosolyme decimo.

Yo el Rey F. R.

VIII.

Los Indios de las Indias Islas son Hebreos.

[*Col. Muñoz, vol.* 42, *fol.* 60 *sq.; en la Biblioteca de la real Academia de la Historia en Madrid.*]

Los Indios de las Indias islas é tierra firme del mar oceano que son el presente del Señorio de la Corona R¹ destos Reinos de Castilla son Hebreos é gentes de los diez tribus de Israel, que Salman Rey de los Asirios captivó é transmigró en Asia en tiempo del Rey Ezequias, los puede haver 2,200 años poco mas ó menos que fueron llevados captivos en Asiria. Este se prueva por cinco razones.

La primera por razon de la habitacion é sitio de la parte del mundo donde se halla que moran é habitan. Esta se funda de una autoridad de Esdras,* donde dice que estos diez tribus de Israel se fieron de alli de Asiria mas adelante muy lejos en una region é parte depoblada de gentes que nunca havia sido habitada, camino de año é medio. Pues caminando desde Asiria dende la Cibdad de Ninive, donde estava Tobias que fue de aquella transmigracion é gente, é los demas de su nacion caminando acia la parte del oriente porque á la parte del occidente no caminaron porque boluieron otra ves á tierra de promision.

A la parte de septentrio é norte no podieron caminar tan largo camino ni á la parte de medio dia, sacando los Sabados é Pascuas que no caminaron los Hebreos, ando á cada jornada veinte millas como los derechos disponen, ó siete leguas que es una milla mas, atento la cuenta de los Cosmografos donde esta Ninive, é el globo é circuitu de la tierra, hecha tambien la cuenta, viene se á concluir tan largo camino á la dicha tierra firme, ó por alli cerca donde se hallan estas gentes que moran, porque tanto andarieron por tierra acá el oriente que los hablan yendo de acá naui-

---

* Esdras, iv. ch. 13.

gando á la parte del occidente. Despues multiplicaronse en la tierra.

La segunda razon es por razon de la multiplicacion é grande numero dellos que es la mayor nacion en numero que hai en el mundo por la grandeza de la tierra que tiene poblada. Esto se funda en una autoridad del Profeta Osea,* donde dice que havian de ser el numero de los hijos de Israel como el arena de la mar.

La tercera es por razon de la lengua é habla que tienen que es Hebraico corrompido, como nosotros hablamos Romance que es latin corrompido. Acá se habla que la lengua de los Indios de la isla Española é Cuba é Jamaica é las otras adjacentes es Hebraico corrompido, é las dichas islas se poblaron antiguamente de la dicha tierra firme, é ansi la lengua destos emano de la lengua que en aquel tiempo se hablava en la dicha tierra firme de donde procedieron. Hallanse muchos vocablos entrellos de la lengua hebrea é en la propria significacion é manera de pronunciar. Las islas é tierra se nombraron antiguamente de los primeros Señores que las descubrieron é poblaron entre ellos juxta illud : Vocauerunt nomina sua in terris suis† é aun los rios tambien, asi pasa aun entre nosotros. Asi Cuba es nombre hebraico, porque por ventura se llamó asi el primer Caçique que la descubrió ó pobló, agora se llama la isla Fernandina, porque el Rey que la mandó descubrir ó en cuyo tiempo se descubrio é cuya fue. La isla Española se llamó en la lengua Aiti, forte a Aisti que es nombre hebraico, porque se llamó asi el primer Caçique que la pobló ó descubrió antiguamente ó por otra causa. Hallanse los nombres de tierras é rios de las dichas islas derivados del Hebraico de hombres ó de mugeres de sus ritos. Caçique en su lengua derivado es del Hebreo Acacin, que quiere decir principio ó altura dellos, porque el Caçique entre ellos es el mas principal é mas alto en lugar é autoridad entre ellos que

---

* Hosea, ch. 2. † Psalms, ch. 49, v. 12.

señorea é manda. Hallanse nombres de hombres entre ellos yones de yona, de Jacob yaque, como nosotros corrompemos, de Jacob decimos Jaque, San Jaque, dicen ellos Jaqui. Samana de Salmana hebreo, é anucia de yona, ures de urias, anaures de anaurias, siabao de siba, maimon de maumon, sibanas de siba anas que son nombres hebraicos. Un rio llaman ellos hayna que es cabe Sancto Domingo en la Española, en Hebraico hain quiere decir fuente. Triste ó lloroso llaman ellos cinoso de Cinoth, en Hebraico quiere decir lloroso ó triste. Azuron cinato quitarsate ha el enojo, en Hebraico acura cinoth idem. Un instrumento de palo que es como porra conque se hieren é aporren llaman te machana, de macha en hebraico quiere decir herida ó ingenio, porque es ingenio ó instrumento para se herir. Hace de pronunciar machana como macana charitas. Los Indios que coman carne humana al tal Indio llaman caribe, derivando de carith que quiere decir occursus ignis, llama de fuego que todo lo abrasa por donde pasa, porque en la verdad estos caribes comen á los Indios é los matan é roban é se despueblan las tierras por causa dellos, é todo lo destruyen é abrasan por donde pasan, como acá llaman á los soldados la langosta ó otro nombre semejante. Hai nombres de las mugeres Ana, Mariam, Sara, que son hebraicos de mugeres. Entre los nombres de los hombres tienen Cahaii de Cahat, Maisi de Moysi. Las barquillas en quel andan en el agua como artesa á la tal barquilla llaman cansa de canu en hebraico, quiere decir stancia en el agua ó porque los sostiene en el agua ó que esta estanca en el agua. El cadalecho en que ponen el maiz ó cazabe ó otras cosas llaman barvacsa, de baaracsa que quiere decir baciralecho. Choa, ayuntamiento, porque alla ajuntan é amontonan las cosas que ponen en el. La pimienta de las Indias llamante axi, de axa que en hebraico suena ó quiere decir furor á cosa furiosa, por el gran calor que tiene é que queme en la boca; le pusieron asi el nombre por el efecto que hace. Hai otros muchos vocablos é palabras entre ellos que en la letra é nombre é significacion es Hebraico, ó tiene mucha semejanza con el, como nuestro Romance con el Latin, que causa brevitatis omitto.

La cuarta razon es: porque todas las qualidades é condiciones é señas que hallan escritas de los diez tribus de Israel en la S. Scriptura, de sus ritos é cerimonias, todas ó las mas se hallan entre estos Indios, en unos mas que en otros segun que despues entre ellos se dividieron en diversas heresias é errores, é sectas é prouincias é cismas que tuvieron entre si guerras, tan largo discurso de tiempo como es dicho. Despues se separaron de Dios, se perdieron la observancia de la ley vieja, é las escrituras é letras que antiguamente tuvieron, secundum numerum quippe ciuitatum tuarum extant dei tui.*

Hallase entre ellos la circumcision, el lavarse muncho todos cado dia en la mar, en los rios, fuentes é aguas; no tocar á los muertos, repudiar á sus mugeres, é casarse con otras é ellas con otros; los caçiques é grandes señores tenen muchas mugeres como se lee de algunos de los Padres del Testamento viejo. Casanse con sus cuñadas quando quejan sin hijos viudas. En la Nueva España é en otras partes sacrifican á los idolos demonios los muchachos, tienen templos altos é sacrifican en los montes, en los arboles, debajo de los arboles sombroses. Tienen la idolatria, el comerse los unos á los otros. Que estava profetizado destos por el Profeta Micha. †

La quinta razon es por razon de lo que estava profetizado deste pueblo en S. Scriptura de la idolatria é pecados.

---

* Jeremiah, ch. 2, v. 23. † Micah, ch. 3.

APPENDIX.

IX.

PREPARATIONS FOR COLUMBUS'S SECOND VOYAGE (1493).

[*Col. Muñoz, vol.* 75, *fol.* 159; *Bibl. de la real Academia de la Historia en Madrid.*]

EL REY E LA REYNA. A vos D. Cristobal Colón ñtro Alm^{te} de las ñtras islas é terras firmes que por ñtro mandado se han descubierto é ha se descobrir en el mar o en la parte de las Indias é á vos D. Juan de Fonseca arced. de Seuilla del ñtro consejo salud é gracia.

Sepades que nos avemos acordado de mandar que se haga cierta armada de algunos navios é fustas para enbiar á las Indias asi para señorear las [terras] de que en nome ñtro esta tomada posesion, como para descobrir otras. Para hacer é pertrechar esta armada é proveer de todo lo necesario, ireis á Seuilla é Cadix é sus dioceses é donde quiera embargaveis navios é mantenimientos pagando sus precios regulares, podreis aprenniar las gentes de todos offc. para trabajar é ir en ella. · Para todo vos damos poder cumplido.

De Barcelona á XXIII de mayo de XCIII años.

Yo el Rey. Yo la Reyna.

X.

THE JEWS AND COLUMBUS'S SECOND VOYAGE.

[*Arch. de Indias, P^{to}* 1-1-11⅔. *Un libro de translados de las Cedulas y Probisiones de Armadas para las Indias del tiempo de los Reyes Católicos, años de* 1493 *á* 1495, *fol.* 2 *vuelto.*]

EL REY E LA REYNA. Conde. El bachiller de la torre nuestro fiscal nos ovo escripto que avia secrestado en poder de ciertos mercaderes desa cibdad quatro mill é ciento é veynte ducados de oro que vinieron en ciertos cambios de portugal de vn judio que hera entonces que se llamaua Juan Bran venissen dirigidos que los pagase á Julian Catanes é Bernaldo Pinolo por cuenta de Antonio de Castro vesino de toledo los quales por algunas cabsas pertenescian á nos é despues nos fue dicho quel dicho bachiller los queria por ser al monesterio de las cuevas desa cibdad por questouiensen alli deposados hasta que nos mandaremos sobre ello lo que fuese nuestro servicio y no sabemos cierto sy los pusieron alli agora por algunas cosas conplideras á nuestro servicio nos serbiamas mandar que los dichos ducados resciba . . . .* para los dar á la persona que por nuestro mandado ha de recibir é gastar los maravedis del armada que nos mandamos hazer para enbiar á las yslas é tierra firme que por nuestros mandado agora se ha descubierto é ha de descobrir en las yndias como vereys por las cartas que sobre ello enbiamos por ende nos vos mandamos que si los dichos maravedis estan en el monesterio de las cuevas vos mandeys al prior é fleyres* del dicho monesterio é agays manera que luego den los dichos ducados como nos gelo escrivimos lo qual procurad por las vias que pudieides, é sy los dichos maravedis estan en poder de qualesquier personas é mercaderes les apremyeys é castrigeys á que luego dar é pagar al dicho. . . .* los dichos quatro mill ciento é veynte ducados de oro ó su valor ó la quantya que hallardes que en su poder fué enbargado é deposytado é dades forma como se sepa la qontya ques é en cuyo poder están é á todo lo que convinien haserle por queste dinero se cobre. Lo haseys é conplys luego en lo qual mucho servicio nos hareys.

De Barcelona á XXIII dias de mayo de XCIII años.

Yo el Rey. Yo la Reyna.

---

* A vacant space in the manuscript. † Freyles.

XI.

THE JEWS AND COLUMBUS'S SECOND VOYAGE.

[*Ibid. Un libro de translados, etc., fol.* 20.]

EL REY E LA REYNA. Conde pariente. Por algunas cosas complideras á nuestro servicio es menester que todo el dinero, oro é plata é joyas é otras cosas que Calderon vuestro maestre, Sala y Collantes vuestros criados, tomaron á Juan de Ocampo alcayde de Vrueña que lo presumia de judio para portogal se traygan ante nos vos mandamos y encargamos que luego hagays dar y entregar y dedes y entreguedes sy falta alguna segun lo veres por vn memorial firmado de Fernando Aluares de toledo nuestro secretario que es treslado del dicho memorial escripto de letra del dicho Collantes firmado de su nombre é del dicho Calderon é de Juan Ortiz vuestro alcayde de alua á Bernaldino de Lerma contino de nuestra casa, é tomad su carta de pago con la qual y con esta nuestra cedula vos doy por libre é quito de lo que asi le dierdes é pagardes y por manera alguna non fagades otra cosa en lo qual mucho plaser y servicio nos fareys y de lo contrario avriamos enojo.

De Barcelona á XX de mayo de XCIII años.

Lleuó Bernaldino de Lerma otro tal memorial como lleuó Diego Cano del dinero é oro é plata é joyas é otras cosas quel conde don Alonso y sus criados tienen y lo han de dar á qualquier dellos.

XII.

THE JEWS AND COLUMBUS'S SECOND VOYAGE.

[*Ibid. Un libro de translados, etc., fols.* 6–9.]

EL REY E LA REYNA. Conde pariente, é por que para algunas cosas conplideras á nuestro servicio es menester que todo el dinero é oro é plata é joyas é otras cosas que Calderon vuestro maestre, Sala é Collantes vuestros criados, tomaron á Juan de Ocampo alcayde de Vrueña en la persona de judios para portugal se trayga ante nos vos mandamos é encargamos que luego lo ſagays den é entreguen é dedes é entregardes syn ſalta alguna segund lo veres por un memorial escripto de letra del dicho Collantes firmado de su nombre é del dicho Calderon é de Juan Ortiz vuestro alcayde de alua é Diego Cano continuo de nuestra casa é tomad su carta de pago con la qual é con esta cedula vos damos por libre é quito de lo que asy le dierdes é pagadedes é por manera alguna non pagades mas otra cosa en lo qual mucho plaser y seruicio nos ſareys é de lo contrario avriamos enojo. De Barcelona á XXIII de mayo de XCIII años.

Quatro taças los tres taçones y vna taça de bestiones	nueve ducados é medio dos florines
vn plantel	quatro cientos é sesenta é quatro reales
mas otro taçon	
cinco pedaços de plata	cinco castellanos é medio
dos cucharas de plata	syete ducados
vn trexillo verde guarnecido de plata	tres justos tres doblas
vna hevilla de plata	dos florines
quinientos reales	treynta é tres marauedis é medio
quatro justos é medio	
catorse castellanos	veynte é seys doblas é media
veynte é cinco doblas	ocho florines

doze ducados
vn espadin
dos axorcas de plata
veynte é una cuentas de plata
dos cerxillos é vnos corales de aljofar
vna cinta guarnecida de plata
dos axorcas de plata
vn çetro guarnecido
trescientos grançadas
dos sortijas de plata
vn joyal é tres anus deys de plata
cinco sortijas de oro
vna cadencya de plata
quatro hilos de aljofar
dos manillas de plata
vnos corales con caentas de plata
dyez é seys cucharas de plata
vna axorca é una manilla quebrada
otro pedaço de manilla de plata
vn taçon
vna cinta guarnecida de plata
quatro taças
ciento é treynta é tres ducados
tres doblas
cinquenta doblas
vn justo
vna cadena con vna cruz de tres brochas la cadena
seys sortijas de oro
vn hilo de aljofar
veynte é nueve florines é medio
ciento é veynte é ocho ducados
diez é nueve justos
ciento é quinze castellanos
sesenta é una doblas
tres sayas, una uerde, otra negra, é otra azul
seys jarros de plata
vn plato de munjur
dos candeleros con sus caños de plata
quatro platales
vn mogil de chamilor
vna carmillona
tres sortijas de plata
treynta é quatro reales
seys doblas
nueve castellanos é medio
dies ducados
quatro justos
dos florines
cincuenta é seys castellanos
cincuenta é cinco doblas
seys justos
mas otro justo
quarenta é nueve ducados é medio
ocho florines é medio
treynta é seys marauedis
treynta é dos doblas
treynta é tres ducados
syete florines é medio
nueve justos é medio

syete dexillos guarnecidos de plata
vn canto de plata
vn çetro
vn vaso de plata
otro çetro
vna calderuela de plata
dos escudillas de plata, la vna de orejas
vn copon blanco
quatro taças
seys cucharas de plata
quynientos reales
setenta é seys reales é medio
mill é tresyentos é noventa reales
cinco hilos de aljofar
treynta é tres cruzados
treynta é nueve castellanos
cient florines, dos justos
vn ducado é medio
ciento é treynta doblas é media
vn justo
doze manillas de plata
vna cadenilla de plata
vna broncha de plata
tres çarçillos de plata
tres axorcas de plata
vna chapa de plata
quatro cubos de plata
vnas cabeçadas de media plata
dos çarçillos guarnecidos de plata
tres bronchas de plata
vn çetro de plata
onze cucharas de plata
quinze botones de plata
vnos caltres é pedaçitos de plata
vn anillo de oro
vn poco de aljofar
dos manillas de plata
vna çinta guarnecida de plata
vnos corales
vn panello de latora de damasco blanco
vnas faldrillas moradas
vn martillo de trontay viejo
vna saya vieja colorada
setenta varas de lienço
mas diez é seys varas de lienço
vna sauana

Calderon, Juan Ortiz, Collantes y se lleuo asimismo el dicho Diego Cano vn memorial de lo que ha de hazer al thenor del qual es este que se sigue:

Por lo que vos Diego Cano continuo de la casa de sus Altezas aveys de fazer en esto. Yr camino dicho al señor conde don Alonso que le hallares en las garrorillas que para el lleuays é recebir el dinero é oro, plata é joyas que vos hara dar el señor conde é yr conello todo á seuilla é entre-

gargelo todo por memorial á Francisco Pinelo para los gastos
del Armada que sus Altezas manda hazer para enbiar á las
yslas é tierras firme que se han de descobrir é han de descubrir en la parte del mar oceano y tomad de Francisco
Pinelo conoscimiento de todo lo que entregaredes y trahedlo
aqui á sus Altezas porque con el se vos descargue todo ello
y aveys de dar mucha priesa en vuestro camino y poner
mucha diligencia é en ello y porque muchas cosas de las
susodichas que asy aveys de cobrad del dicho señor conde
son joyas é otras cosas de oro é plata como veres por el
dicho memorial recibid lo todo y venios á medina y con
personas que dello sepan é ante escribano vendedlas y todo
el dinero junto ó lo que mas dello pudier des aver sy alli
hallardes cambios de personas ciertas para lo dar al dicho
Francisco Pinelo en seuilla en fin de junio ó á mas tardar á
diez de jullio. Recibid las cedulas é enbiad las con correo
propio al dicho Francisco Pinelo y si esto no proueyerdes
desta manera yd vos á lo proueer en la forma de arriba y
en todo poned mucho recabdo é diligencia.

XIII.

THE JEWS AND COLUMBUS'S SECOND VOYAGE.

[Arch. de Indias. See Appendix XVII.]

EL REY E LA REYNA. Fernando de Arcos contino de
nuestra casa. Nos vos mandamos que fagays pesquisas é
sepais la verdad, quien é quales personas falaron una barjoleta con cierto dinero é otras cosas que fue perdida en tierra
de Zamora por ciertos judios al tiempo que salieron de nuestros Reynos, é quien é quales personas tienen qualesquier
piezas de oro de las questavan en la dicha barjoleta.

XIV.

The Jews and Columbus's Second Voyage.

[*Ibid. See Appendix XVII.*]

A el consejo de Olmedo. Nos vos mandamos que las ciento é setenta piezas de oro que teneis de lo que se halló en la barjoleta que se perdió en tierra de Zamora á ciertos judios que la llevan hurtada contra nuestro vedamiento, las dedes é entreguedes por memorial que piezas son á Bernaldino de Lerma para que las dé é pague en la ciudad de Sevilla á Francisco Pinelo para los gastos de la Armada que mandamos facer para enbiar á las Indias.

XV.

The Jews and Columbus's Second Voyage.

[*Ibid. See Appendix XVII.*]

El Rey e la Reyna. Diego de Medina, platero, vecino de Zamora. Nos vos mandamos que todos é qualesquier maravedis, oro é plata é joyas é otras cosas que en vuestro poder estan y dejo depositados por nuestro mandado Juan de Soria, secretario del Principe nuestro, de lo que se tomó que habian dejado algunos judios al tiempo que por nuestro mandado salieron de nuestros Reynos, y antes segund que todo está por un memorial firmado de vuestro nombre, lo dedes y entreguedes luego todo sin falta alguna á Bernaldino de Lerma que es nuestra merced que lo reciba para fazer dello lo que nuestra merced é voluntad fuere.

Estos son los maravedis é joyas é cosas que yo, Diego de Medina, platero, vecino de esta ciudad de Zamora, tengo rescibida por mano del muy noble Juan de Soria, secretario del principe nuestro Señor, pesquisidor y ejecutor del Rey y de la Reyna, sobre las cosas tocante á los judios.

Primeramente que recibi para en pago de doscientos ducados que dio la muger de Diego Guiral, el dinero é joyas siguientes:

P^{re} ciento é veynte é seys ducados que montan   *XIVIIMCCL

Item veynte é quatuor castellanos que montan   XIMDCXI

Item en ducados recebidos y castellanos   XIIM

Item ocho justos á DIXXX cada uno, montan   IIIIMDCXI

Item tres doblas, la una navarresa, montan   IMXCV

Item una corona nueva vale CCCXIC   MCCCXIC

Item treze sortijas que pesaron diez é seis ducados menos quinze granos, la una con un zafir fals, é las seys de oro de florines, é las otras de oro de veynte quilates

Item recibimos un texillo morado de tela angosta con labor, hevilla de plata dorada con doze tachones

Item tres manillas de plata y unas sortijuelas que peso todo veynte é dos reales é medio, é una piedra de diez pistal guarnecida en plata, é un cos

En ocho de Enero de XCIII años recibi de Alonso Rodriguez Zurrador de ciertas cosas que se fallaron en su poder

Recibi de Anton Gomez de Sevilla tres doblos que montan   IMXCV

Item recibi del sobredicho Anton Gomez tres ochavas y un quartillo de aljofar menudo é un centillo de Navarra

En 4. de diciembre de XCII años recibi una taza que pezó dos marcos menos una once é dos trupiñas de seda que no valan nada, é unos coralitos, montó en la tasa   IIIMDCCI

Recibi de un labrador:

---

* The Roman numerals in the margin represent maravedis. XIVIIMCCL = 16,250.

  una dobla é un castellano
  cierta planta bujo
  un camafeo guarnecido de plata
  onze coralitos de gajos
  moneda de cobre que vale   C
  un almizar
  un almojado de seda
  dos telas
  dos cañutos de oro de luto
Recibi de Juan de Bilhorado:
  diez ducados que montan   IIIMDCCI
  los quales el havia traido de judios de
    Portugal á Castilla
Recibi de Anton Herrador de la hazienda
  que se halló en la casa del Aimero de Toro,
  Benito de Chaver, que se averiguó haver
  quedado en su poder de unos judios:
  veynte é cinque doblas, la una nabarresca,
    tasada en un florin   IXMXXV
  diez é seys castellanos, el uno bajo que
    vale 300 montan
  seis curriqués viejos que montan   IIMDCCCL
  trece reales de plata menuda que montan CCCX
Toras
  que recibi de Alvaro de Ledesma:
  ocho toras, las dos de damasco trueño, la
    otra colorada, y otra azul, traidas
Item las otras quatuor de otros colores en
  que la una de ellas es de lienzo,
otro tal que dió Alonso de la Cuba Aleo
cinco toras, la una de seda azul y las dos
  verdes
Recibi de Alonso de Manzars°:
  syete toras de zerzusa viejas, e honze
  pedacitos de seda de una de las dichas
  toras viejas

Recibi
  quatuor tazas de plata
  tres tejillos con sus telas
  sesenta cucharas
  vna sortija de oro de sellan
  syete zarzillos con una sortija de plata
  vn hilo de corales
  vna ropa razagante de brocado raso
  carmin nueva
  dos coberturas de toras, vna vieja de brocado y otra de zarza bien traida
  la plata que se tomó á Iñigo de Ribas Altas que primero se llamaba . . . la qual era de su suegra, judia, que quedo em Portogal
Recibi
  tres briales de chamelote traido negro, é otro de Cotyny, é otro de Londres verde traido
Recibi de Garcia de Janelas:
  tres coberturas de toras, la una de carmesi, aforrada de lienzo azul, descosida, la otra de terciopilo azul, desforrada en paño colorado, la otra de zarzahan de labores, aforrada en lienzo negro roto
  mas una sabana blanca de seda
  una tora como almarizal de lienzo
  las orillas coloradas é los cubos de seda con sus frozaduras
  mas una funda de lienzo con labores de seda
  mas dos corno hazalejas destameña verde, con sus frozaduras de seda é unas labores, é los cubos de desilado
  mas una funda de almadraqueja rota, en que estaba embuelto todo.

XVI.

THE JEWS AND COLUMBUS'S SECOND VOYAGE.

[*Arch. de Indias. See Appendix XVII.*]

EL REY E LA REYNA. Luis Nunez Coronel, vecino de Zamora. Nos vos mandamos que todo el dinero, é oro, é plata, é otras joyas é cosas que Rabi Frain judio, vecino de Burgos, dejo en poder de Doña Isabel Osorio, vuestra muger, segun quella lo manifesto á Juan de Soria, e mas los 4,850 ducados que quedaste deviendo á un judio de unas casas que del comparasteis, lo vedes y entreguedes luego todo sin falta alguna al dicho Bernaldino de Lerma.

. . .

De Barcelona á XXIII dias de Mayo de XCIII años.

Yo el Rey. Yo la Reyna.

un joyal de plata dorado
veynte é quatuor gs° de oro pequeños
tres gs° de oro moriscos
dos hilos de aljofar
vn mondadientes de oro
vna jarra de plata
tres guarniciones de plata de texillos con doze tachones
vna cobertura de alto holera de oro
vna suelta sabadas, que pesa vn marco de plata
vn coranzoncillo de oro
vna caja de tahali
veynte é cinque ducados
tres frutos é medio
vn mantillo do cotay
  dos emboltorios y tres cabezones de oro de camisas y otras menudencias.

XVII.

THE JEWS AND COLUMBUS'S SECOND VOYAGE.

[*This and the four preceding documents, App. XIII.-XVI., are taken from Arch. de Indias P*^{to} *1-1-1⅔.; Documentos inéditos de Indias, XXI. 418 sq.*]

EL REY E LA REYNA. Fern. Nunez Coronel. Nos habemos sabidos y parece por cierta pesquisa, que al tiempo que por nuestro mandado salieron de nuestros Reynos los judios, quedaron en vuestro poder fasta XI marcos de plata de Abraham Aven Rubi, los quales pertenecen á nos, por haber sacado de moneda y cosas vedades de nuestros Reynos el dicho Abraham Aven Rubi: por ende Nos vos mandamos que dedes é entreguedes los dichos XI marcos de plata á Bernaldino de Lerma, contino de n^{ra} casa, al qual mandamos que los reciba á la cibdad de Sevilla á Francisco Pinelo, para paguar los gastos del Armada que mandamos facer á las Indias.

De Barcelona á XXIII de Mayo de XCIII años.

Yo el Rey. Yo la Reyna.

XVIII.

QUEEN JUANA AND THE MARRANOS OF ESPAÑOLA (1511).

[*Arch. de Indias, lib.* 1, *fol.* 120; *Coleccion de Documentos inéditos. Seg. seria* (Madrid, 1890), *V.* 307 *sq.*]

D. JUANA por las gracias de Dios Reyna de Castilla, de Leon . . . delas Yndias yslas e tierra firme del mar oceano . . . Por quanto yo he seydo ynformado que en la ysla española y las otras yslas yndias e tierra firme del mar oceano sean pasado se pasan destas partes muchos yjos e nyetos de quemados a causa de les estar proydido e de begado por leyes e prematicas destos Reynos que no puedan tener ny usar nyngunos oficios Reales ny publicos por los poder aver y usar alla deziendo no estenderse en esas dichas yslas e tierra firme la dicha prematica e provycion e vedamiento, e porque muy merced e voluntad es por lo que a mi toca et atañe que tan bien se estiendan y entiendan alla lo suso dicho et que agora ny de aqui adelante tanto quanto mi merced e voluntad fuere nyngund fijo ny nyeto de quemado no pueda thener ny usar en las dichas yndias e tierra firme nyngund oficio real ny publico visto por algunos del dicho muy consejo fue acordado que devya mandar dar otra mi carta de la dicha Razon la qual quiero que balya por prematica asi como sy fuese fecha e promulgada en cartes por la qual espresamente defiende que agora ny de aqui adelante tanto quanto my merced e voluntad fuere por lo que a mi toca que nyngunos nyn algunos nyetos ny fijos de quemados no puedan thener ny thenga ny usen ny exerciten por sy por ninguna via directa ny yndirecta nyngunos oficios Reales nyn publicos ny concejales ny otros algunos que les sean proyvidos e vedados por leyes e prematicas destos Reynos en esa dicha ysla española ny en las otras yslas e tierre firme del mar oceano so pena que los que tovyesen e usen sin tener avilitacion de nos para ello por la primera vez cagyan e yncurran en pena de perdimiento de los tales oficios, e por la segunda pierda los dichos oficios que toviere e mas la meytad de sus bienes, e por la tercera pierda los dichos oficios que asi toviere e mas todos sus bienes para la camara e fisco del Rey mi señor e padre e mya, e que podamos fazer merced de los tales oficios e bienes aquien nuestra merced e voluntad fuere, e por esta mi carta mando alos nuestro governador visorrey y capitanes e otras justicias qualesquiera que agora son o fueran delas dichas yndias que esecutan e fagan esecutar las dichas penas en las tales personas e oficios e sus bienes que fueren fijos e nyetos de quemados luego que a su noticia venicren e tovieren ynformacion bastante que los que ansi tovieren los tales oficios Reales Publicos concejiles son fijos o nyetos de quemados como dicho es, e porque lo suso dicho sea notorio e dello nynguno pueda pretender ygnorancia mando questa mi cedula sea pregonada por las plaças e mercados e otros lugares e partes acostumbrados desas dichas yslas yndias por pregonero e ante escrivano publico.

Dad. de Burgos a cinco dias del mes de octubre año del nascimiento del nuestro señor de mill e quinientos e honze años.

Yo el Rey.

INDEX.

ABADIA, Juan de la, 36, 37.
Abbas, Samuel Ibn, 14.
Abd-el-Hacer, Jacob, 75.
Aben Crescas, Abiatar, 24.
Aboab, Isaac, teacher of Zacuto, 112.
Abolafia, Juan, 34.
Aborigines of America, origin of, 95-99.
Abraham of Beja, searches for Covilhão, 19, 20.
Abravanel, Isaac, 92, 118; career of, in Portugal and Spain, 52-54; lends money to Ferdinand and Isabella, 77, 78; intercedes for the Jews, 84.
Abravanel, Juda, 53.
Abravanel, Samuel, 53.
Acklin Island, 92.
Aden, 19.
Adret, Isabel, 90.
Adret, Solomon, 90.
Affonso de Castro, Martin, 131.
Affonso V. of Portugal, 26, 53.
Africa, 1, 88, 92; exploration of, 2, 4, 5, 16-20, 111; Inquisition in, 129.
Agreement of Santa Fé, 85, 86.
Ailly, Pierre d', *Imago Mundi* of, 13, 14, 18.
Albacer, Juan de, 67.

Alberto, Carlo, Duke of Genoa, 89.
Albuquerque, Affonso d', assisted by Jews, 119-121.
Albuquerque, Francisco d', 119-121.
Alcaldes, 84.
Alcalá de Henares, archives of, 33, 63, 90.
Alcañiz, the Santangels in, 63.
Aleppo, 20, 131.
Alexander VI., a friend of the Jews, 103.
Alexandria, 1, 114.
Alfonso, brother of Henry IV. of Castile, proclaimed king, 23; death of, 24.
Alfonso IV. of Aragon, 3.
Alfonso V. of Aragon, 63, 64, 75.
Alfonso X. of Castile, 75.
Alfonso XI. of Castile, 75.
Algeciras, siege of, 75.
Alhambra, 30, 58, 82.
Aljoro, Abbot of, 68, 69.
Almanach Perpetuum of Zacuto, 47-51.
Almazan, Miguel de, 29.
Almazan, Pedro de, 30, 36.
Almeida, Francisco d', Viceroy of India, 118.

INDEX.

Alonso, Count, kinsman of Ferdinand the Catholic, 106.
Alonso, Maestre, 95.
Alvares, Alonso, 133.
Alvares, Fernando, 106.
Alvares, Juan, 133.
America, 103, 111; discovery of, 70, 81, 91, 97, 102, 126; aborigines of, 95–99; Marranos in, 127–134; Inquisition in, 129–134.
Amsterdam, 96.
Anchediva, 113.
Andalusia, 21; Columbus in, 12.
Angleria, Pedro Martyr d', 57, 81.
Angulo, Alonso de, 77, 78.
Arabian Gulf, 119.
Aragon, 6, 22, 61, 75, 76; navy of, 1–3; under Juan II., 23–26, 66; Marranos of, 27–30; Inquisition in, 34–40; cortes of, 35, 36, 63; *Justitia* of, 125, 126. See Ferdinand the Catholic; Juan II.
Aragonese, 76; in Columbus's fleet, 89; in America, 123.
Arbués, Pedro, assassinated, 35–37, 66.
Archives, Spanish, 33, 63, 77, 90.
Aristotle, read by Columbus, 13, 14.
Artal, Juan, 30.
Asia, 2, 129, 132.
Astrolabe, improvement of, 8, 9.
Astronomy, studied by Jews, 8, 9, 112. *See* Zacuto.

Atayde, Alexander d', assists Albuquerque, 120, 121.
Avarice of Ferdinand and Isabella, 31, 83, 84, 108, 109, 134; of Columbus, 59, 81, 86, 122.
Avignon, 101.
Avila, Bishop of, 77, 78; sailors from, 89.
Ayamonte, Rodrigo de Jerez of, 93.
Azores, discovery of the, 8; Columbus near the, 100.

BABYLONIA, 63.
Badajoz, bishopric of, 77, 78.
Bagdad, 19.
Barbary, Jews in, 92.
Barbastro, Jews and Marranos in, 36, 60, 63, 68, 69.
Barcelona, 1, 2, 6, 7, 88, 102; Inquisition in, 35, 38, 39; Columbus in, 101, 103, 110, 122.
Barrameda, 129.
Barthomeu, Raymundo, 6.
Beaconsfield, ancestors of, 71.
Behaim, Martin, 9; intercourse of, with Columbus, 12.
Behring Straits, 97.
Beja, royal residence at, 112.
Beja, Abraham of, in Africa, 19, 20.
Beltraneja, nickname of Juaña of Castile, 22.
Benjamin of Tudela, travels of, 2.
Benveniste of Calahorra, 107.

INDEX.

Beradi, Juonato, 110.
Bernal, Maestre, 90, 123.
Bernáldez, Andrés, 81, 87.
Berrachina, Gaspar de, 29.
Berri, Duke of, 26.
Bible, read by Columbus, 15.
Bocrat, Abraham, 47.
Bogado, Tristan, 87.
Bordeaux, 67.
Braganza, Alvaro Nuñez of, 134.
Braganza, House of, 53.
Bran, Juan, 105.
Brazil, discovery of, 116, 117; Marranos in, 129.
Briviesca, Ximeno of, 122.
Bull of Demarcation, 103.
Burgos, Jewish property in, 104, 107–109.

CABALLERIA, De la, family of, 28, 123.
Caballeria, Alfonso de la, 28, 36, 59.
Caballeria, Anna de la, 61.
Caballeria, Bonafos de la, 28, 60.
Caballeria, Felipe de la, 76.
Caballeria, Jaime de la, 28.
Caballeria, Juan de la, 65.
Caballeria, Juana de la, 123.
Caballeria, Luis de la, 28, 29, 63.
Caballeria, Martin de la, 29.
Caballeria, Pedro de la, 26.
Caballero, Diego, 129.
Caballero, Juan, 129.
Cabezas, Alonso de las, 77, 78.

Cabra, Pedro de la, 30.
Cabral, Pedro Alvarez, expedition of, 116, 117.
Cabrera, Andreas de, 27.
Cabrero, Juan, 30, 59, 72, 84.
Cabrero, Martin, 72.
Caceres, 89.
Caciques, 49, 50, 95, 98.
Çacuto. *See* Zacuto.
Cadiz, 88; Inquisition in, 34; Columbus in, 104. *See* Calis.
Cairo, 19, 117, 121.
Cairo, Samuel of, 120.
Calahorra, merchants in, 107.
Calahorra, Benveniste of, 107.
Calatayud, Marranos of, 29, 36, 60, 61, 63, 64, 69.
Calicut, 19, 116, 121.
Calis (*i.e.* Cadiz), island of, 50, 51.
Calle, Alonso de la, 90.
Calle del Coso, a street in Saragossa, 37.
Camacho, revolt of, against Columbus, 123.
Cananor, 119.
Canaries, Columbus near the, 100.
Cape of Good Hope, 113, 129; discovery of, 20.
Cape Verd, 116; discovery of, 8.
Caravels of Columbus, 78, 86, 89.
Carillo, Alfonso, Archbishop of Toledo, 26.
Carlos of Viana, death of, 23, 24.
Carsoni, Jacob, 9.

Cartagena, Jews sail from, 88.
Cartography, study of, 6.
Casafranca, Jaime of, 39, 104.
Castellano, Diogo Ortiz, 9.
Castile, 42, 70, 75, 76, 93; Jews in, 3, 53, 83; under Henry IV., 22-27; Marranos in, 27-31; Inquisition in, 32-35. *See* Henry IV.; Isabella.
Castilians, in Columbus's fleet, 89; in America, 123.
Castro, Antonio de, 105.
Castro, Martin Affonso de, 131.
Castrojeriz, 89.
Catalonia, 1, 2; revolt in, 22, 23, 66; Inquisition in, 34, 38, 39, 66.
Cataluña, 7.
Catanes, Julian, 105.
Cathay, 15.
Catholics in America, 126.
Cea, Duarte Nuñez de, 133.
Celdrán, Pedro, 125, 126.
Cemeteries of Jews, 87.
Cerda, Luis de la, Duke of Medina-Celi, 21, 42.
Cerdeña (*i.e.* Sardinia), 124; conquest of, 3.
Cervera, Jews in, 24.
Ceuta, conquest of, 4, 5; Bishop of, 9, 16.
Chamorro, Moses, 60.
Chronicles, Books of, read by Columbus, 13.
Church Fathers, read by Columbus, 13.
Cifuentes, Count of, 105.

Cipango, 15, 16, 93.
Circumcision among the Indians, 98.
Ciudad-Real, Inquisition in, 34.
Clementes, family of, 60.
Clergy of Spain, 30; taxation of, 31.
Cloth imported from Lombardy, 71.
Cochin, 116, 118.
Cohen, Joseph, works of, 101.
Coimbra, Jews in, 60; Inquisition in, 129.
Colom. *See* Columbus.
Colom, Andreas, 40.
Colom, Blancha, 40.
Colom, Francisca, 40.
Coloma, Juan de, 83, 85.
Colombina in Seville, 13, 14, 17, 48.
Colón. *See* Columbus.
Colonies of Spain and Portugal, 127-134.
Columbo, 131.
Columbus, Bartholomew, 18.
Columbus, Christopher, 8; birth and education of, 11; called Colón or Colom, 11, 40; in Portugal, 11-13, 15-18, 20; relations of, to the Jews, 12, 13, 16-18, 46-52, 54, 59, 81; scientific equipment of, 13-15; goes to Spain, 20-22; negotiates with Ferdinand and Isabella, 40-46, 51, 52, 55-59, 85, 86; fanaticism of, 43, 80, 81, 126; relations of, to Zacuto, 48-51; to Abravanel, 52, 54;

INDEX.

to Santangel, 59, 69-79, 93, 100-103, 123; avarice of, 59, 81, 86, 122; journal of, 80, 81; agreement of, with Ferdinand and Isabella, 85, 86; first voyage of, 86, 87, 91-95, 100; German poem on, 88, 89; fleet of, 89-91; letters of, to Santangel and Sanchez, 93, 100-103; Jews and second voyage of, 103-111, 157-169; disgrace and downfall of, 111, 122; discoveries of, 117; death of, 123, 125.
Columbus, Diego, 20, 55.
Compass, improvement of, 8.
Conference of Salamanca, 45, 46, 51, 52.
Cordova, 37; Inquisition in, 34; Columbus in, 42-45, 55; Junta of, 43-45, 52.
Corduba, Alfonso de, 48.
Coronado, Luis, 133.
Coronel, Luis Nuñez, 107, 108.
Cortes, 28, 29, 32, 62; of Catalonia, 23; of Castile, 27; of Aragon, 35, 36, 63, 64.
Cortes, Fernando, 101.
Cortés, Garcia, 107.
Cosco, Leandro de, 102.
Cosmography, 10, 101, 112.
Costelleto, 101.
Covilhão, Pedro de, explores India, 18-20.
Crescas, Abiatar Aben, 24.
Cresques, Abraham, 6.
Cresques, Azay, 8.
Cresques, Hasdai, 7.

Cresques, Jafuda Lobell, 8.
Cresques, Jehuda, 6-8. *See* Ribes.
Cresques, Solomon, 8.
Cromwell, Oliver, allows Jews to return to England, 96.
Cuba, Columbus in, 93; Luis de Torres in, 93-95; Jews in, 97; Indians of, 98.
Cueva, Beltran de la, 22.
Cufo or Hucefe, assists Albuquerque, 120, 121.
Customs, royal, 34; farmed by the Santangels, 65, 70, 71.

DAROCA, Jews and Marranos of, 60, 61, 63.
Debts due to expelled Jews, 87, 104, 107, 109.
Demarcation, Bull of, 103.
Deza, Diego de, Bishop of Salamanca, 45-47, 51, 52.
Diaz, Bartholomew, reaches Cape of Good Hope, 20.
Discoveries and explorations, Portuguese, 1, 4, 5, 8-10, 15-20, 102, 103, 111-121; Spanish, 1, 70, 71, 81, 91, 97, 100-103, 111, 117, 126.
Domain, royal, farmed, 65.
Dominica, discovery of, 111.
Dominicans, 30.
Don Jehudano, 2.
Don Juda, treasurer of the Queen of Castile, 3.
Don Profatius, 9.
Doria, Andrea, 121.
Duns Scotus, 13.

Durango, Vidal, 36, 37.
Dutch, the, in alliance with the Marranos, 131, 132.

EDICT expelling Jews from Spain, 58, 82-84.
Egypt, 1, 2.
Eli, Leonardo or Samuel de, 35.
Emigration of Marranos to the Indies, 128-134.
England, 26.
Enrique, Cardinal, regent of Portugal, 130, 132.
Enriquez, Beatrice, Columbus's mistress, 55.
Enriquez, Fadrique, admiral of Castile, 23.
Enriquez, Juana, wife of Juan II. of Aragon, 23, 24.
Ephemerides of Johannes Müller, 48.
Ephraim, Rabbi, 107.
Escribano de racion, officer of the royal household, 70, 125.
Española, Marranos of, 90, 127-129, 169-171; discovered, 95; Indians of, 98.
Esperandeu, Juan de, 36, 37.
Esperandeu, Salvador de, 37.
Esra, Abraham Ibn, 9; writings of, 14.
Ethiopia, 18.
Eugene IV., 15.
Evora, Inquisition in, 129.
Explorations. *See* Discoveries.
Exportation, laws prohibiting, 82.

Expulsion of Jews from Spain, 58, 64, 68, 80-91, 104-110; from Portugal, 128.
Ezra, Fourth Book of, 15.

FANATICISM, of Columbus, 43, 80, 81, 126; of Spanish rulers, 43, 134.
Faquin, Juceff, 3.
Farisol, Abraham, works of, 101.
Ferdinand I. of Aragon, 61.
Ferdinand I. of Castile, 75.
Ferdinand the Catholic, 17; birth of, 23; relations of, to the Santangels, 66, 68, 70-72, 75, 76, 78, 123-125. *See* Ferdinand and Isabella.
Ferdinand of Portugal, Prince, 53.
Ferdinand and Isabella, 101, 127; negotiate with Columbus, 21, 40-46, 51-59, 72-79, 85, 86; marriage of, 24-26; relations of, to the Marranos, 28, 29; introduce the Inquisition, 31, 41, 66; war of, with the Moors, 31, 32, 41, 44, 56-59, 72, 76, 77, 84; avarice of, 31, 83, 84, 108, 109, 134; fanaticism of, 43, 134; expel Jews, 80-91; use Jewish property for Columbus's second voyage, 103-110, 157-169; withdraw their favor from Columbus, 111, 122, 123.
Fernandez, Garcia, 56.
Fernandez de Vilanova, Alfonso, 53.

INDEX.

Fernandina, 93.
Ferrara, 101.
Ferrer, Jaime, 5.
Ferrer, Vicente, 60.
Fleet for Columbus's first voyage, 89-91 ; for his second voyage, 104-111.
Fleet-tax of Portuguese Jews, 4.
Fonseca, Juan Rodriguez de, 104, 122.
Fraga, Jews of, 60.
France, 7, 32, 46, 55, 66, 88.
Franchetti, Baron Albert, 89.
Franciscans, 81.
Frankl, Ludwig August, poem of, on Columbus, 88, 89.
Frederick III., Emperor, 15.

Gama, Gaspar da, life of, 113-119.
Gama, Vasco da, expedition of, to India, 112-115, 118, 119.
Garcia, Gregorio, 96.
Gaspar de las Indias, 115.
Gavison, Abraham, 48.
Genoa, 1, 11, 20, 101 ; Duke of, 89.
Genoese merchants and mariners, 71, 91.
Gerona, rabbi of, 39.
Gilbert, Juan, 63.
Ginneu, Benedict, 104.
Girardi, the Genoese, 16.
Giustiniani, Agostino, praises Columbus, 81.
Goa, the metropolis of India, 19, 113, 114, 119-121, 129, 132.
Gold, Columbus's search for, 15, 43, 86, 93, 100 ; in India, 117.

Gómara, Francisco Lopez de, 101.
Gomez of Huesca, Alfonso, 63.
Good Hope, Cape of, 113, 129 ; discovered, 20.
Granada, 85, 114 ; Archbishop of, 33, 44, 77, 78 ; conquest of, 56-58, 66 ; Columbus in, 59, 86.
Great Khan, kingdom of, 93.
Greece, 2.
Gricio, Gaspar, 83.
Guadaloupe, 111.
Guanahani, discovered, 91-93.
Guinea, 5, 13, 17.
Guiral, Diego, 106.
Gurrea, Francisco, 29.
Gurrea, Gaspar, 61.
Gurrea, Pedro, 61.
Guzman, Enrique de, Duke of Medina-Sidonia, 20.

Hamburg, 131.
Hasan, Muley Abul, 30.
Hayti, 98. *See* Española.
Hebrew, the language of the Indians, 98.
Henry IV. of Castile, reign of, 22-27.
Henry the Navigator, 4, 5, 8, 15.
Herrera, Garcia de, 107.
Hidalgos in America, 111.
Hijar, Jews of, 64.
Hispaniola. *See* Española.
Holland, 131.
Hucefe, a Jew, assists Albuquerque, 120, 121.
Huelva, 20.

Huesca, 68.
Humboldt, Alexander von, 5.

IBERIAN PENINSULA, 120, 134.
Ibn Abbas, Samuel, 14.
Ibn Esra, Abraham, 9, 14.
Idol worship among Indians, 99.
Imago Mundi of Pierre d'Ailly, 13, 14, 18.
India, expeditions to, 18, 19, 42, 80, 111, 113-121; Inquisition in, 129. *See* Indies.
Indian Ocean, 117.
Indians, origin of, 95-99, 153-156; oppressed by Columbus, 122.
Indias, Gaspar de las, 115.
Indies, 78, 85, 100; Marranos in the, 128-134. *See* India.
Inquisition, in Sicily, 31; in Spain, 31-41, 66-72, 79, 82-84, 90, 110, 125, 128, 129; in Spanish and Portuguese colonies, 127-134; in Portugal, 128-130.
Interpreters, Jewish, 120.
Inventories of Jewish property, 106-108, 160-168.
Isaac of Sujurmente, 14.
Isabella of Castile, 90, 133; piety of, 32, 33, 43; interview of Luis de Santangel with, 72-79; jewels of, 74-76. *See* Ferdinand and Isabella.
Isabella, island of, 93.
Isaiah, prophecies of, 15.

Israelites, Indians descended from, 95-99.
Italy, 1, 2, 80, 88.

JACA, Jews of, 68.
Jachia, Gedalja Ibn, 47.
Jaen, Inquisition at, 34.
Jaime I. of Aragon, 2.
Jaime II. of Aragon, 3.
Jaime III., King of Mallorca, 3.
Jamaica, 98; Columbus in, 49-51, 111, 123.
Jehuda of Valencia, 2.
Jehudano, Don, 2.
Jeremiah, Book of, 118.
Jerez, Rodrigo de, in Cuba, 93.
Jerusalem, 87.
Jewels of Queen Isabella, 74-76; of other Spanish rulers, 26, 75.
Jews, in Spanish navy, 2-4; in Portugal, 4-10, 12, 17-20, 53, 60; relations of, to Portuguese explorations, 4-10, 17-20, 112-121; nautical science studied by, 6, 8-10, 47, 48, 51; persecuted, 7, 60, 122; in Italy, 12; relations of, to Columbus, 12, 13, 16-18, 46-52, 54, 59, 81; loyalty of, to Juan II. of Aragon, 24; marriage of Ferdinand and Isabella promoted by, 24-26; status and influence of, 27; relations of, to Marranos, 30, 31, 82, 84, 105, 108; provision Spanish army, 52; in Granada, 56; expelled from

INDEX.

Spain, 58, 64, 68, 80–91, 104–110; in Hijar, 64; in Jaca, 68; in Columbus's fleet, 89–95, 111; in Barbary, 92; aborigines of America descended from, 95–99; well-treated by Alexander VI., 103; property of, used for Columbus's second voyage, 104–110, 157–169; in India, 118; in Portuguese and Spanish colonies, 127–134; expelled from Portugal, 128. *See* Marranos.

Jjar, Maria del, 124.

João I. of Portugal, 4.

João II. of Portugal, 53, 111, 112; interested in navigation, 8–10; negotiates with Columbus, 15–18, 55; sends an expedition to the East, 18–20.

Joseph, the court physician. *See* Vecinho.

Josephus, read by Columbus, 13.

Juan I. of Aragon, 6, 7.

Juan II. of Aragon, reign of, 23–26, 28, 61–66, 76.

Juan, son of Ferdinand and Isabella, 45.

Juana, daughter of Ferdinand and Isabella, 128, 133, 169–171.

Juana, daughter of Henry IV. of Castile, called Beltraneja, 22.

Juana, wife of Juan II. of Aragon, 23.

Juda, treasurer of the Queen of Castile, 3.

Judaizers, 33, 39.

Juglar, Gaspar, the inquisitor, 35.

Junquera, S. Perez, 97.

Junta, of João II., 9, 16, 44; of Cordova, 43–45, 52.

Justitia of Aragon, 125, 126.

KAPSALI, Elias, Chronicle of, 23.

Khair-ed-din Barbarossa, 121.

Kingdom of the Great Khan, 93.

Kingsborough, Edward, views of, regarding descent of Americans, 97.

LAMEGO, 19.

La Plata, 134.

La Rábida, Columbus at, 55, 56.

Laredo, Jews sail from, 88.

Las Cuevas, monastery of, 105.

La Seo, Cathedral in Saragossa, 36, 67.

Ledesma, sailors from, 89.

Ledesma, Alvaro de, 106.

Leiria, 47.

Lepe, sailors of, 56, 92.

Lerida, Inquisition in, 68.

Lerma, Alonso de, 107.

Lerma, Bernaldino de, 106, 108.

Letters of Columbus to Santangel and Sanchez, 93, 99–103.

Levant, 18.

Levi, Aaron (Antonio de Montesinos), 96.

Library of S. Pablo in Seville, 96.

Lima, 96; Inquisition in, 133.

INDEX.

Lisbon, 4, 18-20; Columbus in, 12-16, 54; Jews in, 12, 13, 53, 112, 113, 115, 118-121; Junta of, 16, 44; Inquisition in, 129.
Llabrés y Quintana, Gabriel, 6.
Loan of Luis de Santangel, 75-79; of Isaac Abravanel, 84.
Lobon, Fernando Yanos de, 32.
Lombardy, cloth from, 71.
Lopez, Dr., 30.
Lopez, Garcia, 38.
Lopez, Luis, 96.
Lopez, Manuel, 133.
Lopez, Raymundo, 61.
Lopez-Patagon, 69.
Los Palacios, parson of, 81.
Louis XI. of France, 32.
Lull, Raymond, 6.
Lunel, Clara, 63.
Lunel, Pedro, 68.
Lupo, Fernando, 61.

MACHIR, Jacob ben, 9.
Madeira, 128.
Maestre Bernal, 90, 123.
Mahón, 92.
Malacca, Marranos in, 117, 131.
Malaga, Columbus in, 52, 55.
Mallorca, 3, 6, 29, 62.
Mallorca, Jaime of, 5-8.
Malmerca, Nadassan, 30.
Manasseh ben Israel, writes the *Hope of Israel*, 96, 97.
Mantua, 101.
Manuel, King of Portugal, 131, 133; explorations under, 111-121.

Marchena, Antonio de, 46.
Marchena, Juan Perez de, 55-57.
Marco, the surgeon, 90.
Marigalante discovered, 111.
Marranos, 122, 123; promote the marriage of Ferdinand and Isabella, 24-26; status and political influence of, in Spain, 27-30; persecuted by the Inquisition, 30-41, 66-72, 82-84; relations of, to the Jews, 30, 31, 82, 84, 105, 108; in Spanish and Portuguese colonies, 127-134, 169-171.
Marriage among the Indians, 99.
Martin, King of Aragon, 8.
Martinez, Fernando, 16.
Martinez, Garcia, 77.
Martyr, Pedro, 57, 81.
Marzilla, lover of Luis de Santangel's daughter, 61.
Mathematics, studied by the Jews, 5, 9, 46, 112.
Matheos, Hernan Perez, 92.
Mauritania, 4.
Mecca, 114.
Medina, Diego de, 106.
Medina-Celi, Duke of, entertains Columbus, 21, 42.
Medina del Campo, Queen Isabella at, 127.
Melinde, King of, 116.
Mendes de Vascogoncellos, Diogo, 119.
Mendoza, Cardinal of Spain, 26, 57; letter of Luis de la Cerda to, 21, 42.

INDEX.

Menezes, Pedro de, opposes Columbus's plan, 16, 17.
Mercado of Saragossa, 36, 37, 67.
Merchants, Genoese, 71.
Mexico, Jews in, 97.
Milan, 23.
Minorca, 92.
Mohammedans in Spain, 41, 56, 58. *See* Moors.
Molina, Maria de, 3.
Moñiz, Felipa, marries Columbus, 12.
Montemayor, Pedro de, 77.
Montesinos, Antonio de (Aaron Levi), 96.
Montesinos, a clergyman of Lima, 96.
Montferrat, 101.
Montfort, Jaime, deputy-treasurer of Catalonia, 38.
Montfort, Pedro, 29, 36, 37.
Moors, 12; in Spain, wars of, 3, 30-32, 41, 44, 56-59, 66, 72-77, 84; in Tangiers, 53; on Columbus's fleet, 91; persecuted by the Inquisition, 110, 122; in India, 120; in America, 126.
Morocco, 14.
Moros, Garcia de, 36, 38.
Moses, the mathematician, 9.
Moslems in Spain. *See* Moors.
Muley Abul Hasan, 30.
Müller, Johannes, 48.
Municipalities, 29, 62.
Muñoz, Pedro, 37.
Murcia, 90; conquest of, 3.

Nadassan Malmerca, 30.
Naples, 28, 75; Ferdinand the Catholic in, 39.
Nautical science, 112; improvement of, 5, 8-10, 51, 113; seat of, 6.
Naval academy at Sagres, 5, 8.
Navarre, war in, 22, 23.
Navigation, school of, at Sagres, 5, 8.
Navy, Spanish, 1-4; Portuguese, 1, 4.
Nebbio, Bishop of, 81.
New Christians, 31, 130-132. *See* Marranos.
Niña, one of Columbus's ships, 89, 91.
Nineveh, 97.
Noronha, Garcia de, 121.
Nuñez of Braganza, Alvaro, 134.
Nuñez de Cea, Duarte, 133.
Nuñez de Silva, Diego, 134.

Ocampo, Juan de, 106.
Offices held by Marranos, 28-30, 62, 123.
Ophir, gold of, 43.
Orient, tribes from the, in Yucatan, 97.
Ormuz, 19, 20, 120.
Ornaments of gold, not to be worn by Jewish women, 108.
Ortas, Samuel d', 47.
Ortiz, Diogo, 9, 16.
Orueña, Alcaide of, 106.
Oviedo, Gonçalo Fernandez de, 91, 92.

PALESTINE, 2, 15, 114.
Palma, Jews in, 6, 7.
Paloma, Jewess of Toledo, 23.
Palos, 55, 56; Columbus in, 86, 87, 89.
Patagon, Abraham, 61, 62.
Patagon, Lopez, 69.
Patagon, Moses, 60.
Patagon. *See* Pazagon.
Paternoy, Isabel de, 72.
Paternoy, Juan de, 72.
Paternoy, Sancho de, 36, 38.
Patriotism of Jews and Marranos, 24, 52, 70, 71, 79.
Pavia, university of, 11.
Payva, Affonso de, expedition of, to India, 18, 19.
Pazagon, Isaac, 60.
Pazagon, Mayer, 30.
Pazagon, Moses, 124.
Pazagon. *See* Patagon.
Penço, V., 89.
Pension granted to Juan de Santangel's daughters, 63, 138.
Perez, Anton, 38.
Perez de Marchena, Juan, 55–57.
Peru, 97; Inquisition in, 133, 134.
Peruvians, of Jewish origin, 96.
Philip, husband of Juana, Queen of Spain, 133.
Philip II. of Spain, reign of, 131–134.
Pinelo, Francisco, treasurer of Ferdinand the Catholic, 77, 105, 106.
Pinheiro, Francisco, 118.
Pinheiro, Martin, 118.
Pinolo, Bernaldo, 105.
Pinta, one of Columbus's ships, 89, 91, 92.
Pinzon, Martin and Vicente, 87, 91.
Pisa, 1.
Plaça de Trinidad, in Barcelona, 39.
Plasencia, Inquisition in, 35; Bishop of, 122.
Pliny, 13.
Polo, Marco, 2, 16.
Polyglot psalter of Giustiniani, 81.
Porras, Francisco de, conspires against Columbus, 49, 123.
Porto Rico discovered, 111.
Portugal, 103, 109; maritime development of, 1, 4, 5, 8–10, 43; Jews in, 4–10, 12, 17–20, 53, 60, 88, 105, 106, 108, 112, 128; Columbus in, 11–18, 20; explorations of, 15–20, 102, 103, 111–121; Jews expelled from, 128; Inquisition in, 128–130; colonies of, 129–134. *See* João II.; Manuel.
Posen, 114.
Prado, Prior of, 43.
Prester John, 5, 15, 18, 119.
Profatius, Don, 9.
Psalter, polyglot, 81.

QUILOA, King of, 118.
Quintanilla, Alonso de, 42, 45, 70.
Quirago, Vasco de, 73.
Quito, Bishop of, 96.

INDEX.

Rabida, La, Columbus at, 55, 56.
Rabi Frayn (Rabbi Ephraim), 107.
Ram, Jaime, 25.
Ram, Juan, 38.
Ram, Mateo, 36, 37.
Red Sea, 114.
Regiomontanus, 48.
Ribasaltas, Beatrice de, 65.
Ribasaltas, Iñigo de, 108.
Ribasaltas, Juan de, 64.
Ribes, Jaime, 5–8.
Ricci, Augustin, 47.
Rimos, Moses, 6.
Rio del Oro, 5.
Rites of Indians, 98, 99.
Rivers, American, names of, 98.
Rodrigo, court physician of João II., 9, 16, 19.
Rodriguez, Sebastian, 56.
Rodriguez de Silveyra, Diego, 134.
Roldan, views of, regarding Jewish origin of Americans, 95, 96, 98.
Romeral, Juan Sanchez de, 67.
Ronda captured, 41.
Rota, 21, 42.
Rothschild, Albert de, 89.
Rothschilds, 64.
Rousillon, county of, 66.
Rubifrayn (Rabbi Ephraim), 107.

Sabayo, ruler of Goa, 114, 116.
Sacrifices among the Indians, 99.
Sagres, naval academy at, 5, 8.
Sahagund, Juan Alonso de, 107.
Salamanca, 47; Junta of, 45, 46, 51, 52.
Salamanca, Alonso de, 107.
Salmanassar, 97.
Salt-works, farmed by the Santangels, 64, 65.
Sambaya, 18.
Sambenito, 69.
Sampayo, Lopo Vaz de, 121.
Samuel of Cairo, 120.
Sancha, Doña, wife of Ferdinand I. of Castile, 75.
Sanchez, family of, 28.
Sanchez, Alfonso, brother of Gabriel, 29.
Sanchez, Alfonso, a man of letters, 38.
Sanchez, Bernard, 38.
Sanchez, Brianda, 38.
Sanchez, Eleasar Usuf, 29.
Sanchez, Fernando, Infante of Aragon, 2.
Sanchez, Francisco, 29, 36.
Sanchez, Gabriel, 29, 36, 38, 67, 76, 78, 90, 124, 127; relations of, to Columbus, 59, 79, 101, 102, 123; death of, 125.
Sanchez, Guillen, 29.
Sanchez, Juan, of Romeral, 67.
Sanchez, Juan, of Seville, 127, 128.
Sanchez, Juan Pedro, 36, 38.
Sanchez, Luis, son of Eleasar Usuf, 29, 61.
Sanchez, Luis, son of Gabriel, 125.
Sanchez, Pedro, father of Gabriel, 79.
Sanchez, Pedro, son of Gabriel, 124.

INDEX.

Sanchez, Rodrigo, 90.
Sancho, Don, Infante of Castile, 75.
Sancho IV. of Castile, 3.
Sancho II. of Portugal, 4.
Santa Cruz, Gaspar de, 38.
Santa Fé, 84; Queen Isabella in, 56; Columbus in, 57; agreement of, 85, 86.
Santa Fé, Pedro de, 69.
Santa Gloria, in Jamaica, 50.
Santa María, one of Columbus's ships, 89.
Santangel, family of, 28, 29, 59–79, 135–152; persecuted by the Inquisition, 66–69.
Santangel, Agnes de, 67, 68.
Santangel, Alfonso de, son of Azarias-Luis, 61.
Santangel, Alfonso de, son of Columbus's patron Luis, 124.
Santangel, Anton de, 64.
Santangel, Azarias-Luis de, 60–62.
Santangel, Brianda de, 65.
Santangel, Clara Lunel de, 68.
Santangel, Donosa de, 68.
Santangel, Fernando de, of Barbastro, 69.
Santangel, Fernando de, son of Columbus's patron Luis, 124, 125.
Santangel, Gabriel de, 68, 69.
Santangel, Gabriel Gonçalo de, 67.
Santangel, Geronimo de, 124.
Santangel, Isabel de, 69.
Santangel, Jaime de, cup-bearer of Juan II., 65, 66.
Santangel, Jaime de, *escribano de racion* of Ferdinand the Catholic, 125.
Santangel, Jaime Martin de, 68.
Santangel, Juan de, 38, 67.
Santangel, Juan Martin de, 61.
Santangel, Juan Thomas de, 69.
Santangel, Juana de, wife of Pedro de Santa Fé, 69.
Santangel, Juana de, wife of Columbus's patron Luis, 123.
Santangel, Laura de, 67, 68.
Santangel, Leonardo de, 61.
Santangel, Lucretia de, 69.
Santangel, Luis de, burned at Saragossa, 36, 38, 67.
Santangel, Luis de, grandson of Azarias-Luis, 61, 63, 64.
Santangel, Luis de, ambassador of Alfonso V. of Aragon, 63.
Santangel, Luis de, the elder, of Valencia, 64, 65.
Santangel, Luis de, the younger, of Valencia, 65.
Santangel, Luis de, burned in effigy, 67.
Santangel, Luis de, of Calatayud, 69.
Santangel, Luis de, penanced in 1496, 69.
Santangel, Luis de, Columbus's patron, 84; intercedes for Columbus, 69–79; letter of Columbus to, 93, 100, 101; royal favors granted to, 123, 124; death of, 125.

INDEX. 187

Santangel, Luis de, deputy of the Zalmedina, 126.
Santangel, Luisa de, daughter of Juan, 67, 68.
Santangel, Luisa de, daughter of Columbus's patron, Luis, 123, 124.
Santangel, Maria de, 63.
Santangel, Martin de, provincial of Aragon, 63.
Santangel, Martin de, burned in Saragossa, 67.
Santangel, Miguel de, 69.
Santangel, Miguel Luis de, 126.
Santangel, Pedro de, penanced, 69.
Santangel, Pedro Martin de, 61–63.
Santangel, Salvador de, 126.
Santangel, Simon de, 68.
Santangel, Violante de, 68.
Saragossa, 47; Jews and Marranos of, 29, 30, 36–38, 63, 64, 66, 67, 76, 126, 128; Inquisition in, 35–38, 67, 70, 72; Cathedral of La Seo, 36, 67; Mercado of, 36, 37, 67.
Sardinia. *See* Cerdeña.
Sauli, Manuel, 34.
Savona, Columbus in, 11.
School of navigation at Sagres, 5, 8.
Scotus, Duns, 13.
Secret Jews. *See* Marranos.
Segovia, 27, 89; Jews of, 25, 90.
Seneca, 14.

Senior, Abraham, promotes the marriage of Ferdinand and Isabella, 25–27.
Setenel captured, 41.
Seville, 30, 96, 105, 106, 127, 128; Colombina in, 13, 14, 17, 48; archives of, 33, 77; Inquisition in, 34, 110; Columbus in, 104.
Sicily, 6, 25; Inquisition in, 31.
Siguenza, Bishop of, 26.
Silva, Diego Nuñez de, 134.
Silveyra, Diego Rodriguez de, 134.
Simancas, archives of, 77.
Sixtus IV., 34.
Smyrna, 113.
Sofala, 19.
Soria, Jewish property in, 104, 109.
Soria, Juan de, 106.
South America, Jews of, 96.
S. Pablo, Library of, in Seville, 96.
Spain, maritime development of, 1–4; discoveries and explorations of, 1, 70–73, 81, 91, 97, 100–103, 111, 117, 126; wars of, with the Moors, 3, 30–32, 41, 44, 56–59, 66, 72–77, 84; Columbus in, 14, 20–22, 40–59, 85, 86, 122; Inquisition in, 31–41, 66–72, 79, 82–84, 90, 110, 125, 128, 129; unity of, 71; colonies of, 126–129; under Philip II., 131–134. *See* Ferdinand and Isabella; Jews; Marranos.

INDEX.

Spices, Columbus's search for, 15, 86, 93, 94, 100, 111; in India, 19, 116.
States-General. *See* Cortes.
Storms, theory concerning, 51, 113.
Strabo, 13, 14.
Sugar, cultivation of, 128.
Sujurmente, Isaac of, 14.
Sumatra, 117.
Suson, Diego de, 34.
Sylvius, Aeneas, works of, 13, 18.
Synagogues, 7, 27, 109, 118.
Syria, 2.

TABLES of Zacuto, 13, 14, 47–49.
Tacubaya, 92.
Talavera, sailors from, 89.
Talavera, Hernando de, confessor of Isabella the Catholic, 30, 33, 44.
Tangiers, Moors of, 53.
Tarifa, conquest of, 3, 4.
Tarragona, 88; Inquisition in, 39.
Taxation of Spanish clergy, 31.
Ten Tribes, 96, 97, 99.
Teruel, 63; Inquisition in, 35.
Thorowgood, T., works of, 96.
Tobacco, discovery of, 94, 95.
Toledo, 23, 25, 26, 105, 127; cortes in, 27.
Toledo, Fernando Alvarez de, 106.
Tolosa, Dalman de, 39.
Tolosa, Gabriel de, 39.

Tolosa, Luis de, 39.
Torah-rolls, 88, 109, 118.
Tordesillas, Treaty of, 103.
Torquemada, 34.
Torre, De la, a fiscal officer of Ferdinand the Catholic, 105.
Torres, Juan de, 107.
Torres, Luis de, in Cuba, 90, 93–95.
Tortosa, Jews of, 3, 90.
Toscanelli, Paolo, letter of, to João II., 15, 16.
Toulouse, 38.
Trade, injured by the Inquisition, 35; of Marranos in America and in India, 127–130.
Translations of Columbus's letters, 102.
Treaty of Tordesillas, 103.
Triana, Rodrigo de, sights land, 92, 93.
Tribes, The Ten, 96, 97, 99.
Trojan War, 57.
Tudela, Benjamin of, travels of, 2.
Tunis, 113.
Turkey, 88, 114, 129.
Turks help the King of Calicut, 121.

UNIVERSITY, of Palma, 7; of Pavia, 11; of Salamanca, 45, 46.
Usuf, Eleasar, father of Luis Sanchez, 29.

VALCUEBO, Columbus at, 46.

INDEX.

Valencia, Jews and Marranos in, 29, 53, 63-66, 70-72, 88; Inquisition in, 34, 66, 90, 125.
Valencia, Jehuda of, 2.
Valladolid, 123.
Vascogoncellos, Diogo Mendes de, 119.
Vaz de Sampayo, Lopo, 121.
Vecinho, Joseph, 9, 12, 13, 47, 48; opposes Columbus's plans, 16-18.
Venice, 1, 20, 129.
Vera, Pedro de, 36.
Veragua, discovered by Columbus, 49.
Veragua, Duke of, 49.
Verd, Cape, 116; discovered, 8.
Vespucci, Amerigo, 102, 117.
Viana, Carlos de, son of Juan II. of Aragon, 23, 24.
Vicenza, 101.
Vilanova, Alfonso Fernandez de, 53.
Villa do Iffante, 5.
Villaflor, 96.
Villanueva, Angel de, 123.
Villanueva, family of, 60.
Villanueva, in Calatayud, 61.
Villar, sailors from, 89.
Villa-Real, Count of, 16.
Vivo, Miguel, 68, 69.

Vizino. *See* Vecinho.
Voltaggio, 101.
Voyages of Columbus, 89-95, 100-111, 122, 123.

Wars. *See* Moors.
Watling's Island discovered, 92.
Wealth of Jews and Marranos, 28-31, 62, 64, 83, 104-110.

Xamos, Abiatar, 29.
Ximenez, Cardinal, 58, 59.
Ximeno of Briviesca, 122.

Yanos de Lobon, Fernando, 32.
Yelves, Manuel Lopez of, 133.
Yucatan, settled by Oriental tribes, 97.

Zacuto, Abraham, 9; works of, 13, 14, 47-51; relations of, to Columbus, 13, 14, 46-51; in Portugal, 112, 113.
Zafra, Juan Alvarez of, 133.
Zahara captured, 41.
Zalmedina, 62, 126.
Zamora, Jewish property in, 104, 106, 107, 109.
Zapateiro, Joseph, travels of, in Africa and Asia, 19, 20.
Zavalmedina, 62.
Zealand, 131.
Zentolla, a rabbi, 87.

www.ingramcontent.com/pod-product-compliance
Lightning Source LLC
Chambersburg PA
CBHW020908230426
43666CB00008B/1359